Business S.O.S.™

Bring Back the American Dream

What Washington and Wall Street
Can't or Won't Do for Us
We Have to Do Ourselves

Deborah J. Scarpa

deborah@businesssos.com
www.businesssos.com
(305) 586-4022

©2011-2013 by Deborah J. Scarpa

Front Cover:
The upside down U.S. flag is an official signal of distress. It is not meant to be, and is not officially recognized as any type of disrespect when so displayed for the right reasons. To the contrary, here is the relevant part of the US Code of Laws regarding how to fly the flag when in distress:

THE FLAG CODE
Title 36, U.S.C., Chapter 10
As amended by P.L. 344, 94th Congress
Approved July 7, 1976

§ 176. Respect for flag: No disrespect should be shown to the flag of the United States of America; the flag should not be dipped to any person or thing. Regimental colors, State flags, and organization or institutional flags are to be dipped as a mark of honor.
(a) *The flag should never be displayed with the union down,* ***except as a signal of dire distress in instances of extreme danger to life or property.***
Most individuals who have served in the military service of our nation will (or should) recognize this signal.

I believe the life, liberty and property of US Citizens are in dire danger and distress.

Table of Contents

Dedication 6

Acknowledgements 1

Introduction 5

Chapter 1 - The Truth Behind the State of Small Businesses Today 11

Chapter 2 - The American Brand in the Land of Opportunity and Fairness 41

Chapter 3 - Business S.O.S.: Warning Signs and Ways to Get Out of This Mess 66

Chapter 4 - Partnerships, Integration and a Collective Big Think! 102

Chapter 5 - Activism: Your Most Authentic and Effective Marketing Tool for the 21st Century 118

Chapter 6 - How to Keep Up with New Marketing Methods and Social Media 136

Chapter 7 - Bankruptcy is a Scourge for Small Business and Not an Option 169

Chapter 8 - The Way Forward: Ignite Small Businesses and Renew a Sense of Hope 197

Notes 221

Business S.O.S.™

Dedication

To Natalie Scarpa, as a token of my profound admiration and respectful and ardent gratitude for always being there for all of my business and personal trials and tribulations. She is a great entrepreneur who taught me to endure no matter what the challenge.

Business S.O.S.™

Acknowledgements

Many people contributed to the creation of this book. I would like to take this opportunity to acknowledge and thank them for their efforts. To all of them, my thanks.

Research was the key to backing up my entire hypothesis about the current state of small businesses. Without the efforts of my research staff, I would have never been able to substantiate and validate all of the methods and concepts discussed in this book.

I especially want to thank my many research assistants. The first is Taliya Golzar, whose speed and enthusiasm helped me develop a solid outline for the book and a vast amount of data that can be interpreted by the reader whether he has an economic/academic background or is a layperson. I would like to thank Michael Jones for his solid approach to analyzing and interpreting my vision and finding the relevant reference materials that were critical to making this a worthy literary work about the subject of struggling small businesses. His serious approach created cohesiveness to the chapters and his management of the many rewrites was extraordinarily helpful.

My editor, Timothy Staveteig, was kind and supportive as well as an invaluable guide on my journey to writing and publishing my first book. Timothy was able to neutralize my emotionality, while keeping my efforts focused on the bigger picture. His expertise made it an enjoyable experience.

To Tom Oliver, because he is the one employee who stood with and by me, and believed in my concept of Business S.O.S., which was developed through the re-tooling of DJS Marketing to DJS 3S0P (Three Screens Zero Paper). I hope that all small businesses have at least one employee who represents America's past, present, and future work ethic and values. For Tom, my business is more than just a paycheck. He sees the business as a source of inspiration, loyalty, challenge, and growth. The American work ethic was an icon to the world, and when life became only about "the money," nothing worked the same (look at our country now). In Tom's case, it was not what drove him to making this project a source of relief for all of the small business owners we have and will help. For this, I will be forever grateful.

I also want to thank K. Kishore and Kay One Consulting for their financial analysis of countless, troubled companies as well as their efforts to help shed light on how to gain control of company financials critical to facilitating profitability. Their in-put into the feasibility that there could be a place on-line or otherwise to help this important group of entrepreneurs succeed through any economic challenge was very important to the overall concept.

Most importantly, I want to thank my family. My mother to whom I dedicate this book to is an incredible entrepreneur who, like a marine, sucks it up every day through thick and thin and succeeds no matter what challenges the day brings. She has seen it all in her many years of running her business and has never said "no" to any of my requests for guidance and direction.

Many thanks to my brother, Dean, who has given me some very important inspiration for this book. He will read parts of this manuscript and recognize concepts he and I discussed. He never knew that I was formulating them into an action step methodology for small businesses. So, thank you, Dean, for your many observations and words of wisdom.

And, finally, to my family for their support when business was not so great and they had to put up with listening to my new dreams. They always believed that I could turn them into a new reality, for me and so many of my small business colleagues.

My knowledge has been greatly enhanced by all of

Acknowledgements

these people and I am forever thankful that they have all been part of this journey.

Business S.O.S.™

Introduction

I am neither a Rhodes Scholar nor a credentialed graduate of a prestigious school of economics, but I found myself impassioned and qualified to write this book on the state of small business today. Judging from my research, I am not alone in my assessments of our current state of affairs, nor my desire to effect change. Like many of the world's top economists and writers have observed, I find myself one among millions of entrepreneurs who are sick of living in "survival mode" inside this dysfunctional economy.

Most small business owners are just like me - someone educated enough to develop skills in a selected area or areas of trade, but not able or aware of all the "mitigating nuances" in today's markets to incorporate new business models or practices at a rapid enough pace to keep up with our highly competitive, giant, monopolistic corporations.

Having operated a successful advertising agency, I found myself in the perfect storm of today's business challenges. After more than twenty years of doing business with an average revenue of at least $25 million in annual sales and with clients' annual spending levels of $500,000

Business S.O.S.™

to $12 million, I had the proverbial wind knocked out of me in the Great Recession of 2008. This horrific turn of events took my long-standing business to the precipice of near annihilation in a matter of weeks. Of course I had contracts and commitments through 2009, but by the middle of 2009, my business, which was considered one of the most sought after firms in the luxury goods sector, was basically on life support. Clients were calling on a daily basis to cancel work or to reduce their budgets significantly.

While the collapse of the U.S. financial sector in 2008 was the final blow, the structure of small businesses in America had been disintegrating for over a decade. In the case of my business, the bursting of the dot-com bubble in 2000 left me staggering due to lost capital. Then, in the luxury goods industry the terrorist attacks of September 11, 2001, produced shockwaves through the U.S. consumer base that essentially turned off the facet for luxury purchases. In effect, consumers devalued luxury goods in response to such a jolt to America's core. Businesses in New York City--where a portion of my business operated-- were particularly affected by this withdrawal.

At my zenith, I employed 40 people. I had a simply methodology. For every million dollars of revenue I brought into the firm, I needed one productive employee

Introduction

experienced in various disciplines to move the volume of work. This kept me at a very healthy 30 percent margin - a margin that enabled me to earn several million dollars per year. I paid my share of city, state, and federal taxes and still had five million in working capital. I provided healthy salaries and benefits for my highly skilled employee base. However, as a result of the economic shocks throughout the 2000s, my previously thriving business faced a critical threat. As my bottom line became increasingly lean, I scratched and clawed for a solution. But, like most small business owners, we start with a dream and a passion, and just keep plowing forward into the unknown.

We all believed what we read and what we were told - that a great idea mixed with hard work is "all you'll need to accomplish your dreams." This belief in The American Dream as a real possibility is the cultural ideal that has made America the greatest nation in the world. However, Joseph Stiglitz warns in his book, *The Price of Inequality*, that without fairness and balance in our economic systems, a system that is historically based deeply on "American values," the perception of America as "the land of opportunity," our "power," our status, and our standing in the world will be diminished--significantly weakening our markets further.[1]

This "dream", of course for me, had come true. Not only had I operated my business successfully for over twenty years and thought that I would sell or pass my little empire on to my daughter, it had become a machine that I thought was unbreakable unless I decided otherwise. So how is it that after more than twenty years of learning to be a good business stewardess I could find myself in near collapse?

Looking back, I see that the answer lies in the changing structure of the economy. Even prior to the economic downturn, capital markets were drying up for small businesses and technology had rendered business models like my own obsolete. Cheap media alternatives of the Internet and social marketing accelerated these structural changes even faster. Clients had virtually no sales, and therefore very little margin with which to advertise. Millions of small businesses found themselves in the exact situation I was in and this duress continues.

Unlike any other moment in American History, discretionary capital is drying up and it is evident that the changes in our society, culture, technologies, and economies are making many business models completely obsolete. Faced with these quantum changes, we must stop listening to the generic "advice corners" and those that

Introduction

simply pontificate on what can and should be done and rather attack these issues ourselves.

I came to the conclusion that we could change the tides by more of us facing "the truth" and relying on each other to provide whatever it is that each of us needs to excel in our individual, community-based businesses. We could actually resuscitate one business and one community at a time and, eventually, even our country if we establish our own network - A Small Business Network specifically targeted to help companies in S.O.S. This Network would not have the typical bates and switches to creating and increasing revenue. This Network would be without the typical risk to reputations when disclosing personal or proprietary information. This Network would not take advantage of a business in duress in any fashion. This would be guaranteed in writing and based on true American values of helping ourselves by helping each other with ethics and honor. We are calling this network, Business S.O.S.

I have discovered several important alternatives, methods, and resources supporting "how we can help ourselves by helping each other" and will outline them in this book. Taking alternative courses of actions and completely rethinking about how to actually conduct all aspects of business is what re-launched my own business and will be the mechanism to help thousands more finally get out of survival mode and become thriving and profitable.

As I alluded, this book is not an advice corner. Business S.O.S. does not pretend to be a magical cure-all, nor should it be. What Business S.O.S. *does* promote though, is innovative, specialized, and sustainable solutions for struggling small businesses. Further, it is an acknowledgement that each small business is unique and deserves specialized attention and resources that led to the development of the Business S.O.S. Network. As the following pages will describe, this interactive network will form the foundation for a renewed era of small business expansion.

Deborah J. Scarpa
President
DJS 3SOP + Business S.O.S.™

Chapter 1
The Truth Behind the State of Small Businesses Today

This book takes as given that many of our small businesses are in a state of distress. It seeks to lift up the many forces making this the situation. It also offers one solution that, I believe, will relieve that stress and drive economic growth.

I have taken my personal experience and--through the shock and horror of finding myself in completely different life circumstances than I ever planned or expected--have researched and studied how the disconnect between traditional approaches and current needs happened to me and millions of other entrepreneurs around the country. We cannot wait for the toxic economic environment to be restored before we undertake the task of mending and retooling our businesses. We need to find a solution to help others and ourselves. Through my search, I have found some answers and have laid out my findings for public evaluation.

The main aspect of all business is sales. The U.S. market economy has a shrinking middle-class consumer base, and most small businesses trade only in their immediate local or regional markets. We seek out through a variety of methods to cultivate new clients in these markets but find that even with new and innovative ways to communicate the consumers simply do not have the spending capability. Yet, Wall Street and large corporations continue to have growth and even record profits. The complete disconnection between Wall Street and Main Street arises from these basic issues. Why is it cutbacks and downsizing for businesses that are community and regionally based? Why do we hear so much political rhetoric regarding small businesses, but seldom see any action? Why is this not the social imperative of our times? Most importantly, why is there *so little* help? In all of my research, I have come up with a few viable programs and institutions that offer substantive advice and services for small businesses, which is inadequate help relative to the sheer numbers of businesses in survival mode.[1]

Small Businesses are the Majority

The U.S. became the number one powerhouse in the world--and developed a strong consuming middle-class, an ethical productive workforce, and innovative energized entrepreneurs--because of its growth of small businesses. A small business is defined as any corporation or entity that employs 500 people or less. Based on the statistics from the

The Truth Behind the State of Small Businesses Today

U.S. Department of Commerce, Census Bureau, and trends from the U.S. Department of Labor, there are approximately 27.5 million registered businesses in the United States. Of those, 99.7 percent of all employing firms are considered small businesses.[2] I call these the 99 percenters. Consider the following statistics taken directly from the Small Business Administration's (SBA) website: [3]

How Important Are Small Businesses To The U.S. Economy?

Small firms:

- Represent 99.7 percent of all employer firms
- Employ about half of all private sector employees
- Pay 43 percent of total U.S. private payroll
- Have generated 65 percent of the net new jobs over the past 17 years
- Create more than half of the nonfarm private GDP
- Hire 43 percent of high tech workers
- Are 52 percent home-based and 2 percent franchises
- Made up 97.5 percent of all identified exporters and produced 31 percent of export value in FY 2008

- Produce 16.5 times more patents per employee than large patenting firms

Small businesses are the job creators. They currently employ around 54.7 percent of the U.S. workforce and account for 65 percent of new jobs created between 1993 and 2009. Right now, we are struggling with a massive need for jobs. The latest release (October 2013) from the U.S. Department of Labor reports an unemployment rate of 7.8 percent; however, this figure does not take into account individuals who are underemployed, were forced into early retirement, or have dropped out of the labor force because they simply cannot find jobs. Taking all these figures into consideration, we can calculate an astounding underemployment rate of 14.96 percent. That means that there are 23.6 million unemployed and underemployed Americans. It is also reported that only 58% of all able-bodied adults are unemployed in the US as of 2012. Shocking figures for the number one advanced economy in the world. [4]

The Solution

Small businesses are the engine that drives employment, innovation, stability, and growth. The lack of

The Truth Behind the State of Small Businesses Today

focus on small business is a missed opportunity. The figures shown in the previous section indicate that one solution to our unacceptable unemployment lies within this large body of motivated companies. Right now, government needs more revenue to address the already record national debt. Much of our political discourse about small businesses is about tax reduction. Many businesses are not profitable enough during these tumultuous times to be worried about taxes; they would be better served with a redirected government effort. The taxes small businesses have paid historically support our city, county, state, and federal systems, and now all of these systems are in distress. Hence, we hear the call for cutbacks in governmental spending. Yet, the size of government continues to increase. The complete story is what makes our political environment toxic and ever more confusing to the average individual. This idle engine, the small business, could provide the catalyst for recovery. It is simple arithmetic based on the research that if small businesses provide 65 percent of new jobs, then they will generate the supporting revenues for city, state, and federal projects as well. One plus one does equal two key components for decreased unemployment and increased GDP.[5]

Business S.O.S.™

The Invisible 99 Percenters

I think we are all aware of the complexity in the political discourse today. It is well documented that there is more divisiveness in Washington than ever before in our history. I believe the assumption that the Occupy Wall Street movement is a group of leaderless individuals who want a short cut in life is a falsehood. We have all witnessed the argument that they are a disenfranchised group that is not willing to work and do their fair share, but want government programs and subsidies to help them through the tough times. Yet, after reading and seeing many interviews with individuals who are considered occupiers--such as Alexis Goldstein, former vice president of Merrill Lynch and extensive writer on the "Volker Rule," which would ban speculative "property trading"--by our big banks. I believe most Americans are concerned with the same issues: social and economic inequality, greed, corruption, and undue influence of corporations on government. Many of her comments were similar to 63 percent of the country that thinks banks should be regulated. They should not be allowed to be so large that they could again bring down the entire financial system. The "occupiers" where another group that saw and addressed the disparity between 99% of us and the top 1%. [6]

The Truth Behind the State of Small Businesses Today

Many of the occupiers had a profound effect on bringing the frustration we have all been feeling to the national forefront. Having gone down the rabbit-hole myself, the single-most potent issue is this: we no longer share a fair country--a break from the ideal we have all been taught in school. Instead, so much of the economic power of our nation is in the grips of financial institutions, Wall Street and large Corporations.

"Bank loans are the only way most people can dream of starting a business or buying a home. Our biggest banks, drunk on leveraged profits, abused government guarantees to bet against our houses for their own gain, then picked our pockets when it went bad, breaking that bond of trust in our banking system." Alexis Goldstein

This summarizes something that many of us have already thought or experienced.[7]

I believe one of the simplest assumptions in this book is also the most eye opening: most of us are part of these 99 percenters. Whether we call ourselves Occupiers, or Tea Party members many of us agree on some pretty basic issues. If one ventures to be informed, then one would believe, as I do, that this country has stopped being about and for the people. We need to rebalance our political system. We need to invert the hierarchy of power and make some hard choices. The power to make big changes in our economy lies within the focus of this large, highly productive enfranchised group, small businesses.

Shrinking Sales, Shrinking Salaries

In the Great Recession, I saw my company's revenues drop from $20 million to $2, not overnight, but in a drip-drip-drip fashion. I had to reduce salaries paid by my own business, and I witnessed their ultimate effects on families and communities throughout the last five years. I had to pay less to my highly skilled "creatives" simply because my margins were shrinking. As I had to decrease salaries, my own workforce began to do less and less. With less productivity and a reducing demand for my services, I began to see my once thriving, productive business begin to decline. At the same time, without a complete understanding of all the forces at play, it was impossible to evaluate and correct the situation. I can honestly say that after a twenty-year run with very healthy margins, I was clouded by my own success to see that I was in *economic denial*--the inability or unwillingness to acknowledge the real situation quick enough to prevent or change the inevitable.

Such denial--expressed by small businesses--is at an

all-time high. The media adds to this confusion through their emotional discussions, "opinionations," and exposés, making it impossible for the average business owner to extrapolate needed information that could help in their everyday decision-making.

For example, we used to rely on the stock market to give us an indication of consumer confidence. Now, because there is little correlation between the health of our markets and the cash flow on Main Street, I believe the stock market is what has most of us paralyzed and confused. Many of my colleagues still want to believe that they are part of the top 1 percent. This is delusional when you look at the fact that businesses with 500 employees or fewer are considered small and that half of those businesses are based in the home.[8]

Once the majority of us face the fact that we are the invisible 99 percenters, we can work together to resolve and correct what has happened too many of us.

The U.S. is Functioning with Two Totally Different Economies

In a recent article in *The American Interest*, Tyler Cowen identifies two interrelated, but very different American economies. There is a Globalized Trade

Economy in which companies must compete with everyone, everywhere. These multinational corporations have become relentlessly dynamic and brutally efficient. The other Non-Global Trade Economy encompasses a slower pace of change and growth due to a lack of capital, innovation, and a smaller and less competitive trading area with much less growth in consumer demand. This second economy has the capability of producing more jobs, but does not have the productivity gains because of this lack of demand. This is, also, where most Americans actually live and trade.[9]

In general, this is how the two economies compare:[10]

Globalized Trade Economy	**Non-Global Trade Economy**
The GTE is producing the majority of productivity gains, but it is not producing jobs in the U.S.	The NGTE is creating some job growth in the U.S., but very little revenue gains
The GTE has access to an almost inexhaustible source of capital with trillions of dollars in reserves	The NGTE has access to only limited or no capital
The GTE has a larger, faster growing Global Middle Class	The NGTE faces declining numbers of consumers whose incomes are declining as well
For the GTE, life is good and has a relatively promising future	For the NGTE, their mantra seems to be "We're all on our own"

Large, multinational corporations have large capital reserves, smart technologies, and a growing global middle-class to whom they may sell their products or services. Of course, along with all this money, power, and influence, they get to lobby for the most lucrative contracts and policies.

Professor Joseph Stiglitz, winner of the 2001 Nobel Prize in Economics, is a global expert on inequality. He has focused on the U.S. economy in his new book, *The Price of Inequality*. In it, he notes "rent seeking" activities, such as the involvement of the political process to extract "gifts" from the government at the expense of the rest of society.[11]

Rent seeking takes many forms: (1) hidden and open transfers of subsidies from the government, (2) laws that make the market place less competitive, (3) lax enforcement of existing competition laws, and (4) statutes that allow corporations to take advantage of others or to pass the costs on to the rest of society. The term *rent* was originally used to describe the return on land, since the owner of the land receives these payments or resources by virtue of his ownership and not because of anything he does. Countries rich in natural resources like the US are famous for their rent seeking activity.[12]

We are now subject to a variety of rent seeking activities that are seriously affecting the health of our small businesses while perpetuating and enhancing the economies of the Globalized businesses. For example:

(1) High interest rates and trading fees we all suffer from through credit card services
(2) The inordinate amount of fees charged for banking services
(3) Energy companies gaining total ownership of our natural resources like coal, oil, and gas (and we even provide tax payer subsidies on top of this), all the while our own resources are priced according to and sold in the global markets
(4) Public and private companies running our prisons and, now, opening and purchasing schools at lower than market value and then we pay top dollar for their services they provide to our criminal, court and educational systems;
(5) Defense contractors are probably the most egregious as they have little or no competition or oversight in order for the citizenry to even evaluate these high costs.

All of these factors are what has initiated the "too big to fail" paradigm that nearly brought our country to the brink of a depression, and keeps our markets fragile and our growth stagnant. It used to be un-American to be a monopoly; now it is *de rigueur*. Any consultant or business school teaches in basic economics that, anytime there is only one large client or supplier, the system is at high risk should that large entity falter or become insolvent. Further, control of a market from a single firm allows for an unfair allocation of resources. Either way, the results of monopolistic firms bring consumers to their knees. Corporate oversight and antitrust laws were enacted to protect us from these ills. What happened to their enforcement? Small businesses have been seriously injured in this unfair playing field.

The complexity of our current markets without the education, knowledge, and collaboration of all small businesses will be our biggest obstacle unless we act in a strategic manner.

Small Business Could Ignite a New Era of Economic Nationalism

The U.S. is in need of small business revitalization. Part of this is a call for all employees to have a newfound respect for their jobs and the need to work harder than ever, perhaps for less pay. Employers of these small businesses need to dig themselves out of this mess.

American pride and our drive to win have faltered. Yet perhaps it is our pride that has kept us from being adaptive and resourceful. We are thinking that what worked in the past should work in the future. We need to work differently at all levels in order to fight for our country's growth.

Let's put two ideas together. Small businesses, we said, are 99 percent of all businesses in the U.S. and the Main Street economy. In contrast, Globalized Trade corporations are the other 1 percent and have all the growth (think stock markets) and benefits of our economic system. One cylinder of our economy is firing; the other is just pumping along.

Now, let's just focus on the 99 percenters and what we, as a group, are willing to do to save our country and ourselves. I believe there is a strong willingness among Americans to suffer the pains of economic restructuring in order to right this economy for the good of our society. It will be daunting, but when aspiring toward a noble cause, Americans have shown we stand up for what is necessary and right.

Recently, actor Jeff Daniels on the new HBO series, *Newsroom*, addresses this national tragedy through the writing of Aaron Sorkin when asked, "Why is America the greatest country in the world?" When pushed, he replies, "We are not the greatest country…we lead the world in only three categories. One, we have the highest rate of incarceration per capita." In fact we have 5 percent of the world's population, yet we boast 25 percent of the world's prisoners.[13] "Two, we have adults who believe in angels." He does not mention how many U.S. citizens do not believe the data on global warming and a myriad of other scientific facts, and keep themselves inadequately informed or biased towards others' opinions rather than the facts. "Three, we lead in defense. We out-spend 26 leading countries, of which 25 are our allies." We spend more time "nation building" in Iraq and Afghanistan than we do fixing our own infrastructure. Then, he goes on to say, "We *used* to be great! We always stood up for what was right. We fought for moral reasons. We waged war on poverty, not the poor. We aspired to intelligence not belittle it. We explored the universe and nurtured the greatest artists and innovators and the greatest economy... In order to solve a problem, we need to first recognize we have one, and then we could be great again."[14]

    I believe in the body of the 99 percenters, we have the same stuff that made us great in decades past--a will and a drive to do whatever it takes. We need to do what is necessary before it is too late. The strains of an economic restructuring will be painful, but educating and training our workforce, and retooling our businesses simply must occur for future sustained growth. The small business owners, with the help of their employees, have the grit to make it work once again.

Small business owners do not want a hand out, but we would like an even playing field. Many of us do not collect unemployment even when our businesses fail or cannot support our salary. We are willing to work 10-, 12-, or even 16-hour days to figure out how to retool and revitalize ourselves. But, we need to do this together. We need to network and pool our resources so that we can neutralize forces that hold many of us back. Our creative, natural resource is our pride in American ingenuity. Through technology, we can achieve the connectivity we need to communicate--and by instituting a rethinking about how we approach each other as businesses--we can integrate and effect real progress. Business S.O.S. is not just a resume sharing social media network but a place across channels that provides the pro-active tools to fix each and every small business that is in need of resuscitation.

The Truth Behind the State of Small Businesses Today

Five Years After The Great Recession and We Are Still in Survival Mode!

I know we all feel it, those of us in survival mode. Many times each day, it seems, I get phone calls to buy things. I call large firms requesting information. These companies are also in survival mode, and the moment I ask to get help, or at least some direction, my calls are shortened. Potential clients or customers are treated like a numbers game. For every quick contact, they can get 1 or 2 percent sales. Technology is great, but such human robo-calling also creates walls. It is more difficult than ever to break through.

In this book, I am making an appeal to all companies to stop this, network with Business S.O.S., and pool our talents to help other companies--all of us--get out of this mess.

I am also beseeching workers to rethink their approach to ownership. When my business began to bleed, I had employees who had worked for me for over 16 years. Cutting their salaries and benefits was emotionally difficult and, as I referenced before, it did not help; all it did was build resentment. I was literally spending my savings to keep the company afloat. When I tried to explain these financial realities, there appeared to be a disconnect or they simply did not believe me. It was a critical moment for the company. I was disappointed when I found that employees simply did not understand how each small business owner has his or her life in their hands.

Employees are the heart of any business success, and I needed them to outperform during this time. Believe me, I made many mistakes. Surely, one of them was that I did not level with my people and tells them the true state of my own economy. Perhaps I feared a show of weakness in a very competitive market would not be helpful to my business. My competitors could use it to sell against me. Clients need to feel your solvency is assured before they initiate jobs and production.

Small businesses need to realize that it is too late for pretense--the situation is that dire. We need to stop such opaque business practices, face the facts about our own businesses and the economy, and bring back our workforce work ethic and our true American values of helping our neighbors, thereby aiding our country in order to circumvent the fiscal cliff we are facing.

It is painful to accept responsibility. Perhaps your business is doing well. Perhaps you were very conservative with your capital and you retooled and rehired or re-educated your workforce. Could you be a sponsor or volunteer to help another business do the same thing? The networked revitalization of small businesses across the U.S. will reduce unemployment, develop growth in our GDP, and ultimately benefit both those small businesses that are currently struggling as well as the few success stories. This type of social consciousness is the social imperative of our time. Become an activist but this time not for the myriad of great causes but for your country and its basic survival.

The Stats: Five Charts That Need To Be Viewed Together

Part of my expertise is working with media. With mainstream media's deregulation and its fractured, entertainment-based 24/7 news channels, media conglomerates have a platform to communicate any information that draws the highest ratings, produces the highest advertising income, or helps to consolidate their political agendas. With lax FCC regulations, reporting the issues in a fair and balanced manner for the public good is simply passé because it's not profitable. For most small businesses, it is a good part of our continuing education both as consumers and as story ideas.

Hence, these distortions of information from both political parties are impeding a higher level of knowledge and public discourse on all of the issues. It is imperative

Business S.O.S.™

that, as this level of dysfunction in our markets continues, we get the facts right and sift through the information - not to release our frustrations, but to resolve and recast this entire moment in our country's history and see that the health of our small businesses as the catalyst to making our country grow and regain the status of the greatest country in the world.

When viewing these charts, graphs, and information, see that by working together, we small businesses are the majority, the job creators, and the important coalition to change how business is conducted in America. Overwhelming media silence about or distortions of the facts has kept small business owners from seeing themselves and their customers--or even their trading area-- as part of the big picture of economic events. Stocks are up, and everything is fine--no, really. Meanwhile, small business owners remain unaware of the vortex of forces eating away at the foundations of their businesses. As a result, they cannot react to this gnawing damage. The vast majority of us are considered the minions who need to be fed information in a half-baked format, but this does not need to be the panacea. We can work together to inform and assist each other in order for us to effect the big

The Truth Behind the State of Small Businesses Today

changes we need to make. Here are several things we need to know.

1. Small businesses are dying and new ones are not on the rise

The chart below shows that the belief in the American Dream is dying. The land of opportunity is no longer inspiring individuals to take risks and start something new. According to the U.S. Department of Commerce, U.S. Department of Labor Statistics, BED Business Dynamics, with estimates based on 2005 Census Bureau Data, 644,122 new businesses were created. Closures and bankruptcies are based on the total number of businesses that existed at the time, which was 27.5 million. Assuming that the market normally sees losses for a variety of reasons, these figures do not seem that alarming at 565,745 for closures and 39,201 bankruptcies.[15]

Small Business Births, Closures, and Bankruptcies by Year							
	2005	2006	2007	2008	2009	2010	2011
Births	644,122	670,058	668,395	626,400	552,600	440,000	338,000
Closures	564,745	599,333	592,410	663,900	660,900	832,000	1,340,000
Bankruptcies	39,201	19,695	28,322	43,546	60,837	91,000	118,000

Business S.O.S.™

In 2009, we begin to see a sharp decrease in births of new businesses. With nearly half the number of Americans even attempting to start a new business in the years following the Great Recession, the tripling of closures and bankruptcies is an even more disturbing figure. Each political party will utilize these figures to suit their purposes. It is evident that no matter whom you vote for these trends will continue.

Even though small businesses comprise 99 percent, our contribution to the GDP is dwarfed by the massive corporations controlling the financial, health care, and energy sectors. Look at this from a pragmatic standpoint, and you will understand why it is imperative to send out this call-to-action. It is not only important to network our resources in order to pull ourselves out of survival mode; we need to merge these assets to level the playing field, once, and for all.

The next graphs show the drastic increase in bankruptcies in 2012 for individuals and businesses.[16] As I know I am speaking to a group of concerned business owners, this should put the proverbial "Fear of God" in you to see how many of our colleagues have lost the fight. I do not think there is anything more painful or shocking than losing your business. The psychological pain of failure and

The Truth Behind the State of Small Businesses Today

the shock at the speed these bankruptcies are occurring has ramifications on so many aspects of our nation's economic and psychological health.

Bankruptcy Cases Filed/Commenced, Terminated, and Pending (March 31, 2007 – March 31, 2012) in United States Bankruptcy Courts

Year	Fillings	Percent Change	Terminations	Percent Change	Pending	Percent Change
2007	695,575		950,845		1,364,516	
2008	901,927	+29.7	904,207	-4.9	1,284,614	-0.2
2009	1,202,395	+33.3	1,073,619	+18.7	1,418,472	+10.0
2010	1,531,997	+27.4	1,353,528	+26.1	1,596,990	+12.6
2011	1,571,183	+2.6	1,512,011	+11.7	1,659,874	+3.7
2012	1,367,006	-13.0	1,385,725	-8.4	1,641,127	-1.1

Bankruptcy Cases Filed/Commenced by Chapter (April 1, 2011 – March 31, 2012) in United States Bankruptcy Courts

Class	Chapter 7	Chapter 11	Chapter 12	Chapter 13	Total
Business Fillings	32,456	9,616	606	3,588	46,393
Non-Business Fillings	926,301	1,723	---	392,587	1,320,613
TOTAL FILINGS	958,757	11,339	606	396,175	1,367,006

We will talk about it in another chapter, but there is a specific, psychological syndrome that has been identified when someone experiences failure at this level. Not only is this rate of bankruptcies and closures affecting each individual company, it is a trend that is on the rise and has far-reaching implications for our country. If the American ideal of owning your own business is in jeopardy, does this mean there is only growth in localized service providers such as doctors, lawyers, restaurants, and so forth? Or does this indicate that innovation can only be capitalized by large, global, corporations and 99 percent of us eventually become employees? Is this the start of "corporatization" and the decline of our democracy? A concept the economist Schumpeter discussed in his book Capitalism, Socialism and Democracy when elaborating on his theory that democracies would remain fragile when the vigilance surrounding the balance of power between large and small companies is no longer monitored.

The concerns that we are becoming Greece--founded on the amount of our budget spent on pensions and public services--are real. Labor needs to come to terms with this; the pie is being financed and cannot sustain these costs unless there is consensus. We can see that 22 percent of federal spending is on pensions.[17]

The Truth Behind the State of Small Businesses Today

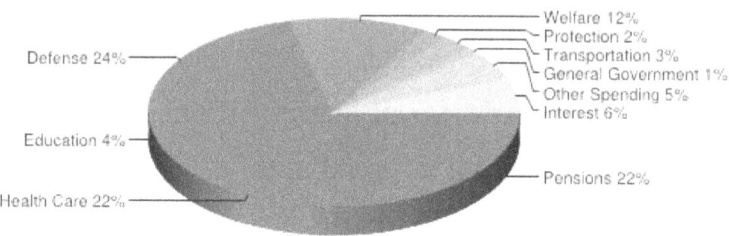

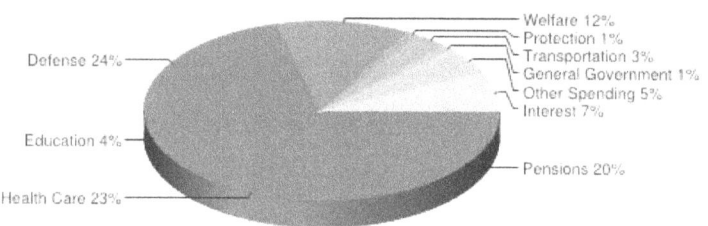

I am confident that anyone reading this book is a self-motivated individual, unafraid of the responsibilities of being an owner and an employer. We simply need the 21st Century methods to restructure these forebodings. It is one of the most stressful experiences to go bankrupt, and, given legislation concerning individual bankruptcies; it can turn a free individual into an indentured slave of his creditors. For most of us, it is not an option, so I offer Business S.O.S. as a viable opportunity to these companies.

Business S.O.S.™

2. The decline in average U.S. incomes

Our consuming middle-class is also dying. With over 46 million Americans living below the poverty line, unemployment high, and our baby boomers moving into retirement, there is simply a shrinking population with the money or the propensity to buy our products or services. As our businesses downsize and lose capital, employees and our own wages, have decreased significantly. I used to make seven figures and had the arrogance that came with all of that buying power. But, like many of you will notice viewing the following chart, I am surely no longer making a million dollars a year as does our top one percent. Further, our top one percent of the top percent is making over $30 million.[18]

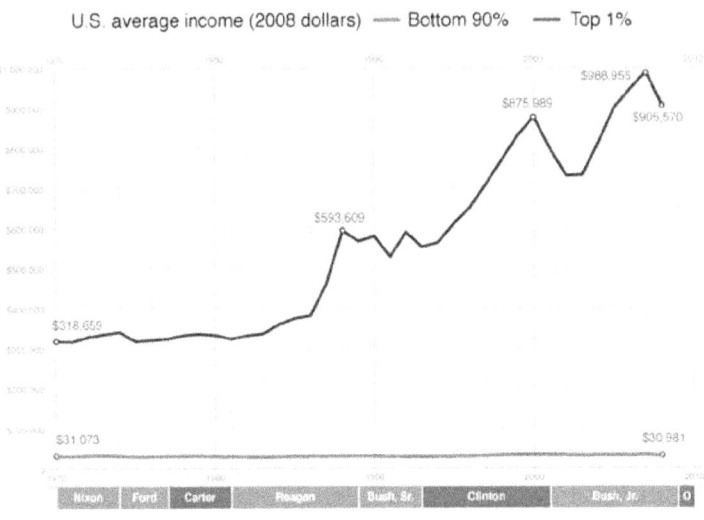

The Truth Behind the State of Small Businesses Today

Here is a clear picture of the disparity between the top 1 percent and the rest of us.[19]

Year	Top 1% Average Income	Top 1% Average Income Including Capital Gains	Top .01% Average Income	Top .01% Average Income Including Capital Gains
2000	886,975	1,282,163	15,275,981	30,223,559
2001	807,323	1,010,251	12,606,207	20,515,521
2002	757,287	886,947	11,625,308	16,524,086
2003	758,111	916,495	12,148,516	18,258,783
2004	836,119	1,085,659	14,688,500	23,864375
2005	924,661	1,257,402	17,195,213	29,421,236
2006	961,856	1,343,876	17,698,914	32,149,872
2007	1,003,791	1,435,002	19,328,745	36,853,470
2008	928,777	1,152,231	17,509,297	27,691,827
2009	814,791	913,451	14,972,931	19,631,207
2010	857,477	1,019,089	16,267,243	23,846,950

I believe many of us have found ourselves in a completely new category. If you are still a member of the top 1 or 2 percent then hopefully, you will see there is something your firm could do to actively assist in the revitalization of small businesses. But if you have seen your wages reduced, or, perhaps, become nonexistent, then I will assume this offer, as a proactive way forward, will interest you.

Business S.O.S.™

In Conclusion: Revitalize our Small Businesses and True American Economic Nationalism and We Will be a Great Nation Again

I have wrapped the story of my own business around current economic times. I have lived through some very painful hardships as a result of this decline in my own success. I had to understand after the shock of the changes in my own microcosm how and why this happened to me. Then, I discovered that it was happening to millions of businesses at the same time across the country. After years of earning and living in the top 1 percent, I found myself in a completely new category. I had to face the reality that I had to identify what went wrong and how I could change it. When I knew I was part of a much larger group, suddenly, I realized the solution. Business S.O.S. was born out of this new knowledge and truth.

We can turn all of this around if we broaden our reason for being entrepreneurs as a means to making money and more about how we fit into the new global reordering of power. When it is only about money, then clearly our economy cannot sustain itself. We need to have a greater and nobler set of goals so that we can assure our country's success as well as our own.

The Truth Behind the State of Small Businesses Today

The goal of this book is to correct this self-centeredness by means of honest collaboration through up-to-date technology. This garners instant connectivity, flattening the globe and gives rise to an era of activism, social consciousness, broader awareness, and a collective big thinking. Things need to change when they brake and the situation with our two dysfunctional economies and the global economy in general is one of breakage. There are vast opportunities to rewrite the rules. Business S.O.S. is a disruptive concept that gives hope, optimism, and empathy toward our small business colleagues. We need to combat apathy with more elevated goals, and not just the ruthless acquisition of money or value to shareholders. This moment has given rise to activist trends in order to make broad and swiping changes to the way things have been done within corporations. Businesses need a way to pay forward to society in order to shape the kind of society we want. One that is not just consumptive but productive and that is not wasteful but is sustainable.

No longer can I just place a product on the middle of an ad and hope consumers covet it as I did in the 1990's. They have to like you. Liking requires way more than just building a product or service; it requires a connection between you and that customer. It is so important that an authentic overture is developed to the consumer you are targeting. I make it a part of all my client's current campaigns.

Business S.O.S. is developed out of this new desire to pay forward and the need to be disruptive in an effort to make swiping changes at a faster pace than what was conceivable in the past. It is for the social good of our nation and is part of a new business model of integration through technology and the social networks that will allow small businesses the opportunities and the competitive edge of larger corporations. I will discuss in further detail in Chapter 3 how it works.

Chapter 2
The American Brand in the Land of Opportunity and Fairness

Redefining the American Brand Through the State of Our Small Businesses

Chapter 1 is a wakeup call for many who own and operate small businesses. If you are in survival mode--conserving cash, not updating equipment, doing only the minimum same-old in marketing and publicity, keeping the truth from employees--then you can derive some comfort in the fact that it is not just you. Yet, so many of us, as owners, blame ourselves and feel like failures--as though we should have known about and planned for such catastrophic losses in 2008, or the dot-com bubble, or even 2001.

America is famous for securing our free markets and providing opportunity to those with a vision and the willingness to take on risk. Yet, small businesses have not been given a level or fair playing field. While the Global Economic players (too big to fail corporations and Wall Street) have been bailed out, we local or regional players (Main Street) have been left behind. We need to restore the balance between these two segments before it is too late and cure the injury to the American brand before it is ceded to other nations.

As a recent *Newsweek* poll illustrates, countries like Finland, Switzerland, Sweden, Australia, Luxembourg, Norway, Canada, The Netherlands, Japan, and Denmark were all listed above the United States in the broad categorization of "The World's Best Countries." Even fifteen years ago, the United States' absence from this poll would have been highly conspicuous; however, events in the international political economy and domestic hubris have chipped away at the American Brand and the attainability of the American Dream. Even now, touting America as the greatest nation in the world is less believable around the world and to its own citizens.[1]

Our research shows, however, that you are not alone. There are 25.2 million of us, and we comprise 99 percent of all businesses. As a collective group, this is a potentially large coalition. Our data also show that our customer base is shrinking and that the nature of our large consuming population is changing. For instance, the Baby Boomers are entering retirement with completely different spending habits than previous generations. How do we find more customers? How do we find success in a changing structural environment? How do we change from "halftime in America" back to that "shining city on the hill."²

Changing the Attitude of Business Owners and Their Employees

This country was founded not only by people but also founded based on an ideal. At the center of these ideals was freedom to work and live as you wish. There is no greater sense of freedom than to work for yourself. Americans commonly regard their society as the freest and the best in the world. Most of our ancestors came across the oceans with little, longing for this freedom in a land of new, open opportunities. We are a nation populated by immigrants who came here to work hard for a better life.

The American ideal of freedom is that all people are created equal and that the role of government is to protect each person's basic rights. In particular, we focus on equal opportunities rather than equal outcomes. Many workers prefer, for example, to work for smaller companies with a healthy work environment over other companies that provide more income, but that demand more from employees.

The disparity in income, the lack of a level playing field in our market place, and an inefficient government bureaucracy--create inequitable opportunities. These are what we need to work together to change and to resolve.

However important these are, it is not the priority in our hierarchy of needs right now, however, as many of us are in survival mode. We are kicking our own cans down the road, hoping we'll have to deal with those issues later when our companies are healthier and when we can work together to force the changes that will benefit the country and small businesses, because we are the majority.

    The top one percent has a better chance of making it than the rest of us. Good for them! Perhaps this group was smarter and stronger than the rest of us, but not for long. The 99 percenters are now aware of their strategies and their transgressions. Out of our own instinct for survival, we need to work together in order to win against a larger competitor. We must find strength in numbers. This is what the new reordering is all about.

    Watching political theatre can make us nauseous when our businesses and security for a better life are in jeopardy. Worse still is what are our children going to think of us when we leave them with the burden of all that crushing debt, on the one hand, and nowhere to turn to earn that money to make the payments, on the other hand. It has been approximated that each American Citizen owes about $54,000 against the Federal Deficit, even our infants, by the end of fiscal 2013.[3]

We have strayed from our ideals, and now we see what we have netted unless we turn back the clock to what we know are true American values. Directly associated to our value of freedom is the ideal of progress: the desire to improve by making use of opportunities. Many Americans can boast that with each succeeding generation, the family's status has improved because they came to America. The classic American family saga is all about advancement. The great-grandparents arrived from the old world with nothing, suffered poverty, and poor working conditions so that they can provide a good education for their children. These ideals are then passed-down to succeeding generations. Through our families and in our schools, we are taught to believe in these ideals that anyone can live a good life and that their dreams can be achieved by hard work, family loyalty, and faith in the free enterprise system. We see from the charts in Chapter 1 that this progress or progression has changed radically.

Unfortunately, reality is teaching us a harsh lesson-- that the American dream is not open to everybody and that our representatives favor those who help him or her get re-elected. Both political parties are guilty of this hypocrisy. Consider such issues as Fanny and Freddy, Dodd Frank, deregulation, the repeal of Glass-Seagull, the debt ceiling, the fiscal cliff, and all the so-called preeminent issues of the day. The causes of our financial dysfunction are clearly the product of both parties' ineptitude and the overriding influence of special interests. How can any of us really know who is at fault? How can these be corrected? Are there so many complex, convoluting issues that confound what is really basic arithmetic?

With a newly found creativity to spin the issues in favor of one political party or the other, it makes it next to impossible to evaluate who is right or wrong. And while we talk about this openly, the hypocrisy keeps poll approval figures for Congress at a record low of 12 percent.

Change of Attitude is the Answer, because Small Business Owners Have the Grit and the Guts to Make It Happen

What has been an effective tool in the past--and one that can be even more effective in the future because of technology--is forming a group, a network, or a coalition. Why? A team of like minds who believe in the same goals and objectives can effect change in a big way. How? Leaderless we can confront our demons and utilize all of our much-needed resources to figure out our own economy. When? This is the inspiration that resulted in the development of Business S.O.S.. By beginning, we are on our own way!

Small business owners are a unique breed of Americans, because it takes grit and guts to start and run a business. In today's world, it takes the heart of a Marine (whether male or female) to face the battles of each passing day. When a business goes into survival mode, it becomes a very stressful way of life. For many of us worrying about making payroll each week, paying our suppliers, or reinventing ourselves in retail-esque environments, every day is a ride up and down a rollercoaster. And when the market sees your company's blood in the water, competitors become vicious, and your customers may be far more aggressive about price and value. When you own and operate a business that is not profitable, and when each day brings the challenges of sales, personnel, marketing, and finance, then one can get demoralized rather quickly.

I never served in the Marines, but I am sure for many of us, it feels like we are going into battle every day in these dysfunctional economic times. We all forge ahead because we must. As small business owners, we never ask for a hand out. Perhaps that is why there are so few government programs for small businesses. Of course, I know there are the Small Business Association, Small Business Development Centers, and small, local outreach

Business S.O.S.™

programs. Yet, try to get someone on the phone when you really need help. It is next to impossible.

I have made a study of all the viable programs available for small businesses, these are all listed, linked and summarized on the Business S.O.S. website (www.businesssos.com). There are approximately 470 federally funded offices to service the needs of 27.5 million companies, a relatively poor network of resources for such a large country. Is this a direct result of our belief in the free enterprise system? Is it the result of a prevailing attitude that business owners are on their own? Just leave us alone and we can make it happen? The unfortunate reality is that success, as the economic cards show, currently, is stacked against us. The complexities of all the mitigating factors make these changes next to impossible for many of us.

Business S.O.S. is not a response to businesses needing a free handout because we do not. Business S.O.S. is a place where business owners can finally acquire information about existing programs and what they can and cannot really do for them without wasting precious time. It is also a place where we can get help or help your neighbor. And through the unique opportunity of advanced technology we can now bring these resources to our distressed small businesses faster and more efficiently.

Do You Need to Send an SOS?

What do I mean exactly? Business S.O.S. will function as a network of businesses in four ways. First, and foremost: if you are a business in distress, we are committed to help you get whatever you need to resuscitate your business if it is still a viable business model for the 21st Century. On the website all you need to do is scroll over the SOS symbol. This will immediately enable you to make contact with us. There will be an SOS hotline as well.

Here we outline our commitment to the distressed small businesses. Our first and most important commitment is confidentiality. Addressing this problem has been difficult because of the consequences should competitors or employees learn about the distress of your company. Hence, unless authorized otherwise, we protect the SOS business's complete confidentiality. Once trust is built, the SOS business will likely need to connect to relevant resources that could assist this small business.

Our second commitment is to be a resource available to businesses. It is also not a bate-and-switch approach, in which the distressed business is asked to join with undisclosed or additional cost. We will offer a true resource for businesses to gain the help they need when they need it. At first, we will launch in specific cities. Later, we plan to go national, and we will connect with other businesses that are willing to help the most needed or most critical.

Sponsors

If the distressed companies are not paying an up-front or payment over time, then how will Business S.O.S. keep its doors open? We turn to corporate sponsors, members, and individual volunteers. Small and mid-size businesses have embraced our old fashioned, American ideal of helping our neighbor. By means of digital technology, sponsors may be located in your city or region or perhaps across the country. It is a powerful, timely call to action to help your colleagues and in turn help yourself. Such action provokes additional action and progress, which are vital to changing the negative trends in which we are now entangled.

What does a sponsor gain from his or her benevolence? The sponsor gains invaluable internal and external PR. Such reputation cannot be invoiced in a commercial sense. However, such sponsorship can be noted as part of a company's commitment to helping others. I believe the true value will be participating in this great moment in time of which we are all a part, and the good feelings that come from helping your fellow American out of his or her distress and in turn helping yourself and your country.

Sponsors are companies that have the knowhow, technology, financial acumen, services, human resources, construction for modern physical plants, communication equipment, smart machines, green technology, marketing, transactions, legal, quality control, equipment, transportation, production of all types of products and services, experts in various fields. Business S.O.S. will provide each company in SOS access to a variety of companies that have signed on to provide real help--and not just advice–to our struggling small business neighbor.

Our Volunteers

Volunteers will be another, primary asset of Business S.O.S. Not all Business S.O.S. members will be owners or operators of a business that can provide direct retooling or service to struggling businesses. Some will come from organizations with a specific expertise. Individuals who have worked in various aspects or key disciplines can assist our businesses rectify critical areas for our businesses so that they can pull themselves out of survival mode and into thriving mode for the challenges ahead.

This type of network developed at the grass roots level in every one of our communities can effectively change the course of events not only by helping each individual business to regain control but also by putting control back in the hands of the people who are willing to make these important attitude changes for themselves and their country.

Let's Accept the Hard Work and Pain in Order to Get Back Our Country

I always told my staff that control is freedom and that freedom is happiness--a very simple equation. With the lack of leadership in Washington and their obvious inability to enact sensible, helpful policies--and I am pointing my finger at both parties--we need to get our small businesses functioning and producing so that we can pay the taxes that are needed to pay for our city and state services, educate our children, and pay down this debt. It sounds painful but how about it is also the noble thing to do.

We all do it every day when we sit down and develop our own budgets. No thinking person would run up their debt as destructively as our government and large banks have done. Our government has simply refused to make the difficult decisions necessary to remedy this cumulative illness. Small businesses are creating the largest portion of the jobs in American and with this newfound energy could create an even greater amount than ever before.

Business S.O.S. is for all of those companies and committed Americans who are proud to play by the rules of fairness because those rules do work. As we watch all of this lack of transparency and accountability, in the end, we will all lose... even the Global Trade 1 percenters. Bad ethics drives good ethics out, but we are determined to set the example of what being a true American is really about.

Real progress matters to us because it is a pivotal part of our ideals. We want to work hard and get scrappy to do the little things that will make a difference. None of us needs government help because we can and will help ourselves. We can rely on our team of small businesses to be there and help each one of us figure it out and then to be there to support us for the long hall.

I am sure all of us have supported a friend or a relative when they started businesses by offering advice and by buying whatever they sell. That attitude of community needs to be resuscitated. The pride in our hard work, and the ethic to produce high quality products and services are so important. These must be restored.

Bring Back American-Made in a Big Way

I am in Miami and admire how so many Cuban Americans have contributed to American ingenuity. The label "American Made" means something. Think about how things have changed. Things were not made of plastic; they were made with stainless steel. Permanence has given way to one-use and disposable. There is real brand equity that we forged during our country's growth. Back when we fostered and established American products as having a higher quality standard than most countries. This was born out of our ideals in which products were made with integrity. We are all aware that American manufacturing is again on the rise. This is a point of departure for many companies to examine the viability of returning their production to the homeland instead of out sourcing jobs overseas. Labor here may cost more, but the quality standards just cannot compare. In a recent article in *Wired Magazine*, Brenda Koenner states that, "one reason to abandon China is quality: some products are too flawed to sell."[4]

For many U.S. firms, the decision to manufacture

overseas is a no-brainer. Labor costs in China and other developing nations have been so low that as recently as two years ago, anyone who refused to outsource was viewed as a dinosaur. But, China now has seen a rise in wages and demands from their own workforce, so the bargain it once was is now up for serious evaluation. For the small business that makes up the largest sector of innovators in the U.S., it is time to rethink this business model of taking their production and supply chain to the other side of the world. But retooling is costly. How do these companies find the manufacturing facilities here in the U.S. or capitalize their own businesses for this production? Business S.O.S. wants to fill this gap at a rapid pace through integrating our sponsors and members.

Many of us have heard about how the Emma Maersk and Wal-Mart's four-monster container ships every week deadhead to China empty of goods. I could point out that this is contributing to our $273 million trade deficit. Instead, I want to ask how small businesses and a revitalized American production system can fill those ships. With a revitalized sector of small businesses and workforce, this could be a point of opportunity. Yes, I am against the power of conglomerates like Wal-Mart when we elect officials and put up with our campaign finance structure as it stands today so that they reap all the benefit of globalized trade agreements. We need a place where our voices and votes can be heard and counted, and we feel strongly that this vehicle could be Business S.O.S.

Our trade imbalance is undoubtedly unsustainable. I realize that all of our officials in Washington may not be educated in the more complex issues within the discipline of economics, but surely, they are aware of these basic facts. Yet, when examining all of the trade bills passed in the last 30 years, it is evident that lobbyists had their hands in blinding our officials into ignoring these basic premises. Despite this error, we can change that equation by developing trade to suit the purpose of our small businesses.

We Need to Create a Real Call-To-Action from Our Employees

Right after September 11, I saw a big drop in revenue as a result of this horrible event on American soil. The switch simply turned off for the American consumer. The "I have got to have" era of the 1990s turned into "Show me its value" It was like a great basketball game stopped and the momentum just never got back to the same rhythm. Right at this time, I was blessed with a beautiful baby girl. I needed to refocus for the first time in my 20 years of owning and operating my business. For many of us, these are the standard distractions that can make or break your business.

The company began to have one or two months a year when we would spend more than we took in (bleed). Then it occurred more and more often, as the luxury sector felt continued stress. During that time, I began to dip into my savings and stock portfolio to make payroll. I would tell my employees please work hard because I am investing my daughter's future in this company. How could I down size? That would show my competitors I was weak. How could I let people go who were loyal to me for 16 years? So I consequently did what I thought was the right thing, but in the end was the stupidest thing I could have ever done. I was, in effect, working for my employees. They were holding the keys, but, instead of working harder or smarter, they instinctively sensed my demise. Everyone began to worry about their own skin and, in so doing; productivity and service quality went down. They lost their jobs anyway as a result. Many of my employees are still looking for work.

Lesson learned because many owners feel they are working for their employees, and employees just do not get it. My strongest message for employees working for a small business is...work hard. These are tough times. Go back to the old school of thought, like "an honest day's work for an honest day's pay." Enough freelancing on the owner's time, like visits to YouTube and Facebook. Be conscious of your daily contribution, because your country needs to see an up-tick in productivity. If you do a study on the search-term *motivation*, America ranks last in a Google Search. No one is interested in the term *perhaps*, because no one is motivated to know more about it. We need to buckle-down, change our attitudes, and get energized. What better way than to help your neighbor and your country to break this yoke of a flat Gross Domestic Product (GDP)?

How Do We Take Advantage of Globalization for Our Small Businesses?

To many Americans, globalization and technology have crippled their small businesses because they simply do not have the know-how, and the smart machinery, to bring their products or service to the global marketplace. We see large corporations outsourcing everything from their production to their call and collection services to markets like India, Indonesia, and China.

There are two perspectives. Even though it is important to understand the imbalance of our trade deficit, it is also an opportunity to examine globalization and how not just large businesses can capitalize. Thomas Friedman is one of globalization's ardent followers. His understanding of this new globalized market is something of which all small businesses should be cognizant. He defines *globalization* "as the inexorable integration of markets, transportation and communication systems in a way that is enabling corporations, countries, and individuals to reach around the world faster, deeper, and cheaper than ever before." This integration is what we are striving for with Business S.O.S., which makes globalization part of the method that will help specific small businesses find new customers or new resources enabling them to get out of this trend of just surviving. Yet, globalization needs to be managed for the good of all companies.[5]

    Just like other fragile concepts such as democracy, it takes a vigilance to keep them secure from degradation. This applies to our approach to globalization. What would America look like if our representatives carefully studied the policies for trade and were cognizant when these policies tilted in favor of conglomerates like Wall-mart? They should set standards for shared globalization and trigger mechanisms to stop too much import and stimulate more manufacture to export products evenly and fairly. Friedman goes on to say that everyone is affected by this new system of globalization, but not everyone is benefited by it. This concept of managed globalization is an important issue because as multinational companies grow and get stronger in their integration they are able to produce more capital than some countries and the balance of power will then change from our sovereign countries to corporations. What a world that would be?

What does this mean to you and your small business? According to Thomas Freidman, globalization is fundamentally misunderstood in the Unites States. He feels strongly that our political leaders are not explaining globalization because it is a political lightning rod. Yet, not to explain it leaves the small businessman out of what Friedman calls a fundamental paradigm shift.

Take for instance my small business, which did business with the Italian Trade Commission jewelry division for years. Looking back, I can see that I received this coveted contract because so many American marketing firms were not venturing out into the globe for business, as business was so flush and supposedly safe in the US. This experience allowed me to develop the skills and human resources necessary to become profitable while working with a foreign entity. Unfortunately, this sector has dried up because of the desperate situation Italy is now in economically. This set back does not negate the fact that I have learned to communicate and service companies globally and have developed Business S.O.S. utilizing these techniques and technology

    Friedman goes on to explain further how torn both parties were in discussing globalization: Democrats were debating whether the North American Free Trade Agreement was a good thing; and the Republicans put duct tape over the White House Chief Economist Greg Mankiw's mouth when he said outsourcing might be a good thing. It means that with the right human resources and smart technology, many of your businesses could integrate into the global market in order to achieve growth. Sound thinking would facilitate a sector focusing on American-made and another sector could distribute these products and services globally. These two approaches need to be fostered by a support team that could help determine the best scenario for each individual business. This big shift in the world--that is moving away from a vertical model to a collaborative horizontal model--is a point of opportunity we must help small businesses explore.

    Leo Sun, at BusinessDictionary.com, talks about the

effects of globalization on small business. He references the classic story about a small town grocer who gets, mercilessly, taken out by Wal-Mart. The grocer had an established customer base, but simply could not match the low prices offered by Wal-Mart. In fact, Wal-Mart has sprawling global resources and is willing to sacrifice margins to take out any local competition wherever it goes. In the end, customer loyalty means nothing, and the grocer goes bankrupt, decades of hard work decimated seemingly overnight. This is the impact of globalization on small businesses.

Now view it from the other side. The large multinational companies take full advantage of the perks of globalization such as outsourcing, uneven exchange rates, and low margin high volume sales models. This makes them nearly impossible to compete against. Mr. Sun goes on to say that the lesson for small businesses like the grocer is:

- Sell something different
- Align yourself with other local businesses
- Consolidate your resources
- Fight back against this unfair playing field

These types of alliances are difficult to forge for

most business owners because many of us have never developed this type of collaborative skill set. Business S.O.S. has developed the tools and technology to promote these relationships within your trading community, regionally, nationally, and even globally.

Redefining the American Brand

Globalization is a direct result of information technologies (IT) and our ability to travel and communicate to a multitude of offices and facilities around the world. It increases our free trade and opens new markets. It is global economic integration that will enable all businesses even small businesses to foster opportunities. We simply need the proactive vehicle to enable small businesses to understand fully how it could work for them.

The effects on the American brand are far reaching. Because so many companies now outsource their product production to a multitude of countries, it places a greater burden for these companies to hold true to their American values. One of the main resources we are exporting through economic integration is civil and political freedom by communicating our democratic ideals of a free society. The platform for this exportation of our values is through our corporate governance both within and outside the U.S.

Business S.O.S.™

Through the efforts of small business networks and constituencies, we can develop from the ground up the type of American leadership that the world has envied and aspired to for two centuries. The world as a whole is just as backward as the U.S. in overcoming the complexities of globalization. By tearing down borders and barriers, globalization can and will have a positive effect on small businesses.

In Conclusion

Chapter 2 discusses how principles and ideals have been the foundation for our powerful economic growth for the past two centuries. Our historical focus on the development of human potential and on progress--these are what have always set us apart as a nation. The question is how we keep those ideals intact as we evolve into a globalized nation at the small business and in many times the individual levels. What progress now means is unclear.

Since the melt down of Wall Street, the power and influence of our capitalistic markets has declined. We need to retain leadership in and control of our free markets. We need to lessen the imperialization of our corporations around the globe. We need to reverse the declining middle class. In sum, the essence of our American brand needs to be re-evaluated. The task is to press the re-start button on our economic engine and create a strong sense of economic patriotism. For individuals and companies, the task is to create a culture and system in which the focus is to uphold the basic ideals of our free and fair society.

Power comes in the development of these new relationships. We need to lead again, and we invite others to observe how we structure our corporate governance. The transforming of these ideals converts what is intangible to something of value. If we create such a movement through small businesses now motivated out of necessity to venture into the global market, we will see the powerful trust-building process that occurs in any office after a certain amount of time. This office would become the global office.

Chapter 3
Business S.O.S.: Warning Signs and Ways to Get Out of this Mess

The Great Recession is not over--at least not for many small businesses. They remain in survival mode, and this could make an already slow economic recovery even slower if we do not get it right. Small businesses have traditionally led rebounds.[1] As we discussed in Chapter 1, until 2008, small businesses employed over 50 percent of the U.S. workforce.[2] While some report that this number is increasing, it actually has been dropping due to closings or bankruptcies of so many small businesses.[3] This number will continue to decrease unless we do something about it.

The economy's effects on small businesses have been catastrophic. Over the four-year period from 2009-2012, we have seen over 5.8 million bankruptcies.[4] Most owners of these businesses are still out of work, aggressively looking for ways to resuscitate their businesses or start something new. This has resulted in an identity crisis for many small business owners over the age of 50. It has also resulted in the drastic decrease in new start-ups by younger entrepreneurs. Because of the decrease in the number of businesses opening in the US–and the

Business S.O.S.: Warning Signs and Ways to Get Out of this Mess

increase in the percent of closures and bankruptcies--it is easy to understand the reason that so many young talented entrepreneurs hesitate to establish or attempt to maintain something that has almost a 85 percent chance of failing. These statistics are unprecedented in the history of our great nation.

I have been president of a mid-size successful advertising agency for over 25 years. With my business model obsolete and limited capital to retool into a significant digital agency, I was stuck taking less desirable accounts just to stay afloat. This can be a demoralizing situation for many who found themselves re-launching their business or trying something entirely new. Reinventing yourself at 40, 50, or even 60 years of age can be daunting. The "entrepreneur adrift" is an under-reported story of the aftermath of the Great Recession.

For businesses that have survived, owners find themselves in the daily battle to keep revenue flowing, all the while trying to control increasing overhead costs. These businesses cut expenses to the bone. And business owners who are still operating under immense psychological pressure will, again, be pressured anew by clients who are reducing or even freezing their budgets. There are so many problems today that many people simply want to get out.

However, this is not an option for most with the job market as it is. As Shakespeare wrote, "Uneasy lies the head that wears a crown."[5]

In a recent article in *Forbes*, Scott Shane outlines the unusual high loss of jobs from businesses closing versus the gains from new businesses startups. Shane writes that in the 1990-1991 downturn, business failures destroyed 103,000 more jobs than were created by new businesses startups.[6] In the 2001, the difference between jobs destroyed from businesses shutting down and jobs created from start-ups was 209,000.[7] In the time span between 2008-2009 the Great Recession, the net loss was 800,000.[8] This data erodes our confidence in the American dream.[9]

That the Great Recession resulted in greater job loss from business failure and much less job creation from company formation than any previous recession cycle is bad enough. Yet, this was also more concentrated in small businesses than ever before (as seen in the following graph).

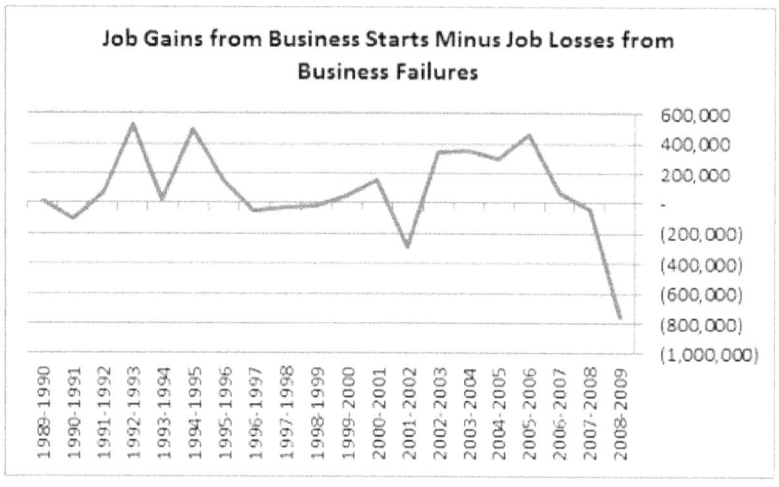

SOURCE: http://www.forbes.com/sites/scottshane/2012/04/29/hallmark-of-the-great-recession-job-loss-from-small-business-closure/

Small loans (less than $1 million) to small businesses continue to shrink, falling to $613 billion at the end of FY 2011.[10] The dollar value of small loans is down substantially since the start of the financial crisis and the Great Recession, and that downward trend remains. Without capital, how do we keep going or even retooling? The SBA data reveal that the inflation-adjusted value of these small business loans shrank by 19 percent between 2007 and 2011.[11] There has been no recovery in the real value of small loans to businesses, so the financial system we bailed-out is simply not there to reciprocate this help for small businesses. Much of this is a result of the decline in real estate lending.

Business S.O.S.™

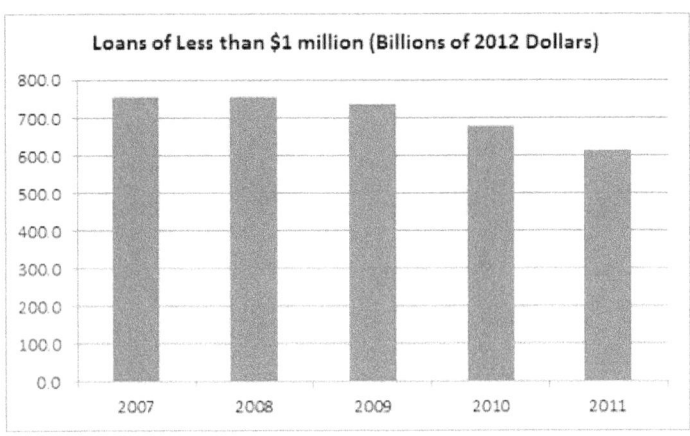

SOURCE: Source: Created from data from Small Business Economy 2011
http://smallbiztrends.com/2012/04/the-great-recessions-effect-on-small-loans-to-business.html

The impact of these broad-spectrum, structural changes is damaging--even catastrophic--because of the way in which they linger. The suffering is affecting millions. With cash reserves stretched, capital assets become collateral for borrowing, which is the kiss of death for some as they over leverage their situation. Yet, this is the position in which many companies find themselves in order to try to survive the sheer length of time the economy stays in this state of meager growth.

With our understanding of the deep, structural changes to the economy in the wake of the Great Recession, the collapse of many small businesses is no surprise.[12] However, even when there exists a general cloak of economic doom, each company's struggle and collapse show unique aspects. The following case studies, which were compiled by Eilene Zimmerman, lift up the distinct differences in *every* small business.[13] Understanding the uniqueness of each small business is what propelled Business S.O.S. to develop a flexible, specialized solution for every struggling company.

Company: Wesabe

Wesabe was a personal finance business based out of San Francisco. Wesabe was a web-based company that allowed individuals to budget their money online. They received almost $5 million in venture capital funds and exceeded 150,000 customers in their first year of operation. However, less than a year after Wesabe's creation, a large competitor entered the market. The competitor was a company called Mint, which provided the same web-based service as Wesabe. But Mint's consumer interface was easier to use and the design was better. After losing more and more customers to companies like Mint, Wesabe shut down their operation in 2010. Although they had customers interested in their service, they simply did not a user-friendly product.

Business S.O.S.™

Company: Gotham Concierge

Gotham Concierge was a Manhattan-based business that ran errands and handled simple tasks for clients. As the economy faltered in late-2008, Gotham Concierge began to lose many clients for whom a professional concierge was simply a luxury. In response, Gotham invested heavily in advertising--but to no avail. The owner and founder, Alison Kero, noted that not only was the advertising a waste of valuable resources given the situation, but also that she simply did not love what she was doing. In the end, Alison lacked the drive to persist through poor economic times.

Company: iParents.com

While Facebook was still foreign to many middle-aged adults, iParents.com offered an online community for parents and families. This website sought to provide methods for parents and families to coordinate schedules, make plans, and interact. However, iParents.com began to focus too heavily on fancy applications on their website (like schedule-based text-alerts). The owners of iParent.com spent too much of their working capital on this fancy development and on expensive marketing campaigns aimed at drawing venture capital. By straying from their original focus, the owners of iParents.com clouded the foundation of their business, ultimately leading to its failure.

Company: Large Format Digital

Large Format Digital was a Wisconsin-based company that printed advertisements on the side of trucks. With a booming business since 1998, Large Format Digital invested in their own installation facility in the mid-2000s in order to save on production costs in the long run. However, there often, organization "redesign" is used synonymously with organization "re-structure." However, organization redesign is much more than moving boxes on an organization chart. Organization redesign is about aligning the key performance levers (structure, processes, roles, people practices and measures) to ensure maximum performance and achievement of the organization's business strategy. It is leadership's responsibility to 1) allocate tasks and responsibilities, 2) organize formal reporting relationships, and 3) facilitate communication. It is important for a leader to pay attention to the organization's design because that is what employees pay attention to; it defines how the work is allocated and divided, how communication flows, and ultimately, who someone's boss is.

Business S.O.S.™

The Time is Now!

The case studies cited are an example of the urgency to create an alternative to bankruptcy or closure--a place, digital or otherwise, where small business owners can catch their breath before they let go of all their investments in time and money. Business S.O.S. will provide an in depth online questionnaire to determine whether a business is in the fragile state of "Save Our Ship," the SOS distress call for aid from others. Then, through the help of our community of Sponsors, Volunteers, and Experts, we can determine how we can prevent these companies from failing or continuing to struggle. We cannot afford to ignore our neighbors' suffering and the pervasive tragedy of the destruction of our American dream.

As Companies Fail, Consumerism Falls

As companies fail, there is always an overriding effect on consumerism. As the lack of confidence remains, spending--which drives two-thirds of the U.S. economy--stays dormant.[14] The general effects on most businesses, large or small, are that sales and profits decline.

First, the business owner cuts back from hiring (or even lays off once critical staff). Second, in an effort to cut costs and improve the bottom line, businesses stop buying equipment and stop producing new products or innovation that require costly research and development (R&D). Marketing and advertising expenditures are also cut. Third, the customers of these companies begin to pay slower, partially, or not at all. Fourth, even this tactic drains critical funds. So these companies borrow against assets. Fifth, debt from delinquent payments affects a company's credit. These changes in credit rating result in higher interest for loans or credit cards. Sixth, one of the results of this credit crunch and declining revenue is that companies cut their staff. Seventh, the morale of the remaining employees also begins to suffer and that takes its toll on productivity. Wages do not increase, though prices of gas and consumer goods have all increased during the recession and cause even more discontent.[15] Eighth, other aspects involve the goods and services produced by these distressed companies--they suffer from quality control. In turn, these products or services may then suffer even further as their desirability in the market decreases. Now these eight steps spread. As firms seriously impacted by the recession spend less money on advertising and marketing, media companies from whom they used to order get squeezed and the cycle repeats.

    Looking back, I can truly relate to this, as my firm

Business S.O.S.™

was one of the largest print media-buying firms in the Southeast. Firms like mine have seriously affected the bottom line of large media companies in every division. As these effects ripple through the economy, it becomes even clearer that Washington and Wall Street simply can't, or won't, help us. Facing all of these problems and more, I realized that the rise and fall of my firm was just one more microcosm in the vast global macrocosm connecting many of us in this dysfunctional financial funk. Faced with all of the challenges and frustrations of this moment in time first created denial, then lethargy, then shock, then anger, and now innovation and passion.

  A deep psychological syndrome infects entrepreneurs and subsequently, their employees--many of who are in a defensive mode, clinging to their jobs. I became obsessed with finding an adequate resolution that could effectively help others get the lifeline they so desperately need after five long years of being in survival mode. Because I was there on the front lines, I could see the overriding problems and then work to find a solution. That is called innovation. Thomas Friedman states that "continuous innovation is not a luxury anymore--it is becoming a necessity."[16]

  In sum, Business S.O.S. was born out of a dire need

to revitalize our small businesses. America's economic future could be at the precipice of how quickly we can respond to the needs of small business entrepreneurs.

What is Business S.O.S.?

Business S.O.S. is defined by its name: a place, digital or otherwise, where small businesses can truly get the help needed when in financial or professional distress. These businesses likely have their own personal resources and know-how in order to resuscitate their business. They need a lifeline because nothing they have tried has worked. This is not their fault, but due to the unusual economic circumstances in which we find ourselves.

I decided to take on the hard task of writing this book because I had succumbed to the financial disease and because no matter where I turned there was no real help other than bankruptcy, closure, or a complete change in business model. Luckily I found the way forward. Yet, small business owners need to be careful. Bankruptcy is no longer an option since the changes in the laws in 2005.[17] Bankruptcy stays on your credit report for ten years. And in this new age in which partnerships are going to be a key business tool to rebuild, no one wants to partner with a company that is not solvent.

For these reasons, bankruptcy should be avoided at all cost. This is one of the main issues for so many small businesses in survival mode. Bankruptcy is no longer a lifeline to remaking a floundering business vibrant again. It is no longer a rope or lifeline for transitioning into a different business. Businesses need to be pulled away from drowning in debt and distress. Bankruptcy, which I will discuss in chapter 7, is a "scourge" not only because of these new laws and policy to protect large institutions but it is a terrible and humility complex legal process that can leave an entrepreneur psychological traumatized for many years and a much worse financial position than before this complex filing. It has become a brutal process and many lawyers sell bankruptcy as the only way to get a clean slate and then the veiled legal difficulties one can become embroiled, could take years to unravel at a great cost.

Business S.O.S. will be that support arm necessary to resuscitate any business from going over their own fiscal cliff. As of this date, my research reveals little or inaccurate information online about resolving your business debt through bankruptcy. The concept of bankruptcy was developed around "creative destruction" as a natural result of capitalism and risk taking. Bankruptcy is one of the most complicated areas of the law yet thousands of lawyers misrepresent in it as a "fresh start" in order not to scare off their potential clientele. Unfortunately once revealed many small business owners find themselves worse off. And, frankly, when you are short of cash, you tend to engage the legal and accounting services we can afford, and not necessarily what we need. Many times attorneys do not explain properly the ramifications of such a serious filing as bankruptcy, and many times these cases blow up in the face of the innocent, suffering business owner. Individuals such as Donald Trump or large corporations can file for bankruptcy protection because they have a legion of lawyers to protect them and a group of financiers ready to reorganize the debt. But the small business owner most times does not have this level of assets, and I seriously urge anyone thinking about bankruptcy to contact us first, not to receive legal advice, but to acquire the resources necessary to circumvent such a catastrophe.

The Warning Signs You are in SOS

As defined in Chapter 1, survival mode is when you have cut staff, cut salaries, stopped R&D, and cut overhead expenses, in order to hold on until the economy improves. But this recession has slogged on for a long five years, and there seems to be no end in sight.[18] Once you are

Business S.O.S.™

functioning at the bare minimum and the bleeding does not stop--*bleeding* is when revenues taken in for a period do not cover your expenses–you are clearly in SOS.

Step 1. In any effective evaluation, the first step is to prepare or review accurate financials. So often I have spoken or read about turn-around experts, or bankruptcy attorneys that do not even look at financial statements in order to get an accurate picture of the distressed companies financial status. Don't let this happen to you.

Many companies in survival mode cut corners so deeply that they no longer have access to adequate accountants or accounting. Business S.O.S. will provide this service digitally with special login privacy restrictions. Without an accurate financial statement, you are flying blind and probably closer to crashing than you realize.

Business S.O.S. will be programmed to connect distressed companies to high-level volunteers and resource companies automatically through proprietary software. The Business S.O.S. team will vet these resources in advance. The distress signal will be put out into the market place anonymously along with a description of the problem and tasks. Companies and volunteers within our network will be alerted, and they will initiate contact with our distressed business owners. Hence, the business owner has access to experts for free or at a fraction of the usual cost. It also will help during critical time periods when research is sometime hindered by a lack of knowledge or paralyzing stress. Let's face it. We all know how to run a business when times are good. It is totally different when the tides have turned and enormous pressure is upon a business owner to resolve a multitude of critical issues with little or no capital.

In turning around my own company, I have developed a unique skill set for strategic rethinking. I speak freely about my own firm because, after the sheer outrage of trying to figure it out without any real proactive programs, I was compelled to think outside the box to creatively service my clients in a unique manner. Please learn from my mistakes. Not only did I lose my controller and my accounting staff in order to cut costs, I began to hire inadequate help who simply were the right salary but did not have the skill set to keep me informed in the manner in which I had been used to for over 20 years.

In the stresses of trying to run a failing company, many of us suffer a variety of psychological symptoms that few understand or recognize. It is something like a fog or malaise. Imagine me, after running a highly successful company for over 20 years; I find that no one has the revenue for print media. A certain denial began to set in and a refusal to accept this quantum change after 25 years. Even though I was in development to retool my company to a digital agency, I feared if I really looked hard at those financials, then I would completely melt down or give up. So many of us have done this. After years of being master of my own ship, I was failing, and I simply could not face it. After suffering terrible losses I began reading and hearing so many sad stories that it left me no other outlet than to communicate this unique, under-recognized and under-reported tragedy affecting so many small businesses across our country.

Where do you go when you're 40, 50, or even 60 years old and your business fails? How about adding all of the business owners who have closed or ceased operating if they are counted in the unemployment or under-employment figures? It was recently reported that 63 percent of all able-bodied workers in America are not employed. You can count on the millions of hard working business owners who were not able to survive as part of that large group. Where are these individuals today?

Step 2. Next, you need to evaluate your customer base. What is the quality of your customers? Or, to focus thinking, from which customers do you not like to hear? Perhaps these customers are not worth having. They might place too many demands on your time or endlessly negotiate prices or deals that do not cover your costs. Yet failing companies desperate for revenue often hold on to them or take them as clients out of desperation for cash flow. This often perpetuates a downward spiral.

    This, of course, is another horrible mistake I made. After September 11, the jewelry sector that had enabled me to build my luxury goods business simply went flat. I regrouped and entered advertising/branding for the real estate sector. (Perfect timing right before the bubble burst, but during the time when they where spending millions on advertising.) I became one of many small businesses upon which many real estate developers prey. It was during my tenure at securing some of the finest real estate developers as part of my client portfolio that I began to struggle. I think this method of these developers is known but never reported or exposed because of their power and strength. Their method is simple and legal. They create unnecessary complicated accounting requirements in order to stall payment. They audit and re-audit. They pay you when their construction loans release or they tell you to hold until that happens. Hence, small subcontractors finance large multimillion-dollar global developers. And then, many times, they simply do not pay or they hold your payment so long that you take out loans because they are too far into your receivables. Meanwhile, you are too afraid or unable to hire the caliber of attorney or take action to stop a job because they will cripple you with lawsuits. These methods are very hard to fight against. As I retool, I will never take a client who cannot pay net 30 days consistently. Yet, during survival mode many small businesses are saddled with these bad clients.

In becoming a Business S.O.S. member, you will have access to strategic consultants who begin the process of evaluating your market and determine who, what, and where that market is in the 21st Century. Perhaps if you are a small local company you need to develop and retool to become a regional company. Yet, many small firms--with the aid of technology--can become a national or even global enterprise. All of the tools and resources will be made available once this is determined through the Business S.O.S. network.

Step 3. Are you controlling your costs? In today's market, the cost of everything is increasing, but clients want it produced for less. That is simple arithmetic and for many of us it just does not work. This cost versus profitability needs to be evaluated. Driving the bottom line through revenue growth is the greatest challenge in today's economy for small businesses. If you are not growing, you are dying. But what if even with small spikes in growth we could control our costs. These small incremental opportunities could help in the long run to save our ventures. In my business at the very start of the downturn, I found that I became uncompetitive because of my bloated overhead. The episodic slashing and burning that became necessary in order to survive really damaged my company. Controlling costs for small ventures is where a lot of the risk is taking place now. How do you re-tool and re-staff or train and know when and how to sustain these imperative operational focuses without tipping over to insolvency while trying? As a result of innovation in IT, there are many ways to take wasted steps out of a variety of businesses whether they are service oriented or industrial. The need to re-evaluate is another area that has changed dramatically in the past few years as a result of the high speed and intensity of changes that all of our companies will continue to under go. A one size fits all is an obsolete model. When it comes to terms and turn. You can reduce your working capital to zero if payment terms were matched with inventory turn of each service or item produced. New ways to work with vendors is to ask them to keep title to their inventory or utilize staff on a freelance basis. Why sit on inventory if it is not contracted or accounted for. In the case of my business, it became mandatory that I not develop a large infrastructure and carry all the salaries as I did before because it is difficult to control when work is not at a consistent flow. This is why it is advantagous to create unique partnerships and teaming in order to concentrate recourses when they are needed and to cut this cost rapidly when it is no longer necessary. In trying to get out of survival mode, we need to control costs by forging high-quality partnerships--relationships that are flexible and easy. This growing need to execute fast partnerships for projects or on an on-going basis will be expanded in Chapter 4.

With so many lawyers in the world, these partnership agreements or contracts are generally inadequately written. We have done the research and offer several partnership agreements that should withstand the scrutiny of protection. However, no contract is foolproof if the people undertaking the relationship are not honorable. Many lawyers say contracts are meant to be broken. We need to re-educate ourselves and stop listening to attorneys who thrive on arguments; instead, we must let our behavior and ethics guide us through this change in corporate culture. With so much blood in the market, there are a lot of happy, thriving law firms. This simply should not be the case going forward.

Experts should be consulted when determining overhead costs. These strategic decisions will be authored by a team of experts assigned to the businesses on survival mode. A simple spreadsheet can master the way ahead. A well-laid plan is necessary in order to facilitate the way out of survival mode.

Step 4. What you need next is a true understanding of the state of your human resources and the ability of you and your management during these tough times. So many of us fall short. It was so easy for me on the way up, but on the way down it is difficult to make good decisions and problem solve the obstacles with clarity and vision. When you begin to fail that once-driving confidence is also severely damaged. Many of you, I know, are completely demoralized from the state of your business and finances. Money is not everything, but it is important for the wellbeing and stability of our families. As it goes for individual small companies, so it goes for our nation. We have lost sight of what good leadership is and how--just by reinvigorating the old passion and love for our work--could help many companies begin the process of this new business climate.

Think of Business S.O.S. as a lifeline someone from a ship has cast to you. Your hope is restored; your enthusiasm for life is renewed. The Business S.O.S. network will unify and ignite the former excitement of entrepreneurs to meet the challenges of these quantum changes in our business environment. Each member--whether it is a volunteer resource company, sponsor, or company in survival mode–will be required to confirm they have read our corporate governance preamble: that we are a group of individuals who aspire to help each other through our toughest days; and that our business relationships are forged on trust and a sense of community. By so doing, we create excitement and hope for the future.

Step 5. Now you need to get control of your cash flow. If cash is king, then controlling it is queen. But how do we do that when margins are so low? With the economy still dysfunctional, the year of liquidity will be slow in coming unless we take drastic measures. Cash flow is the blood that keeps the heart of your business kingdom flowing. Cash flow is one of the critical components of success for a small business. Many a profitable business on paper has ended up in bankruptcy because of the amount of cash coming in doesn't compare with the amount going out. This of course is easier said then done when a company is in SOS. I use myself as an example. After the financial crisis of 2008 money evaporated rapidly. I like many of my small business brethren cut cost dramatically but needed working capital to increase contracts in order to increase cash flow. This was extremely difficult to leverage, as it cost me anywhere from $5,000 to $25,000 to pitch an account. I aggressively went after accounts and lost thousands of dollars doing so because no one was advertising.

"Despite the fact that cash is the lifeblood of a business---the fuel that keeps the engine running---most small business owners don't have a handle on their cash flow," says Philip Campbell, CPA and former Chief Financial Officer and author of "Never Run Out of Cash". He goes on to say: "Poor cash-flow management is causing more business failure today then ever before."

In a recent Equifax data report, it was found that bankruptcies among the nations 25.4 million small businesses leaped by 81% between 2008 and June 2009 and continues to climb. Lack of capital is the main reason for business failure.

What is SOS Small Business Redesign?

When an overwhelming challenge presents itself, people step up to do the job that needs to be done. This works well in a crisis. However, on a day-to-day basis, we count on organizations to ensure that the right people and resources are in place. A well-designed organization helps a leader move beyond "fighting fires" toward a strategic, long-term focus. Many of our businesses--like mine did--need just about everything. This includes a complete restructuring of equipment and IT, physical plant, human resources, systems analysis, more rapid and sophisticated accounting practices, training and reeducation of current staff, and critical partnerships that reduce cost and create revenue.

The most important thing to understand about organization redesign is that there is no right or wrong organizational design. Organization redesign efforts are all about balancing tradeoffs. That said there are some designs that would make an organization more effective than other designs. Effectively designing an organization involves both science (gaining clarity on what you need your organization to accomplish) and art (combining all

Warning Signs and Ways to Get Out of this Mess

organizational elements into a coherent design).

Next, the greater the clarity provided or the reason for the redesign effort, the greater the potential for success. There are five major reasons that would indicate an organization redesign effort might be necessary:

1. Shifts in the organization's business strategy (e.g., required change in core product due to competitive influences)
2. Renewal of the work environment (e.g., introduction of new technologies and impact to work flow)
3. Cultural/political changes (e.g., current culture interferes with performance)
4. Staffing/resource changes (e.g., need to do more with fewer people, or need other skill sets from your people due to IT and economic climate)
5. Dysfunctional or non-functional design (e.g., Ωpoor coordination, excessive conflict, unclear roles, poor work flow, etc.)

Often, a leader will want to use a redesign effort as a way of either getting rid of problem performers or

Business S.O.S.™

retaining top performers. While this is a common reason for reorganization, it is not the basis for the method of redesign at this critical moment in our country's financial predicament or instability in the company being redesigned. The pressure it puts on the organization and the potential for selecting an optimal design will be the key to the success of our Business S.O.S. concept.

To determine the best design, evaluate each option against the goals set for the redesign effort. There are a variety of options for organizing the top layer of the organization. You can design around function (e.g., Operations, Marketing, IT), customer (e.g., Pre-teens, Older Adults), geography (e.g., Northwest, Southwest, foreign countries), or a combination of these. The best approach is to brainstorm options and then rate each option against the goals to be set. This way, you will be able to understand the tradeoffs and make decisions about the shortcomings with which you can live.

For example, one project I worked on was to correct staffing issues that had come up when I had to retool my own firm. We had collaborated with effective creative placement firms we felt had good talent evaluation skills and furnished us with an in-depth criterion for each candidate. As a support organization, they have become an invaluable arm to access rapidly new talent pools. In terms of the overall corporate redesign, we collaborated to help the group come to a consensus on a new design that would work for all areas. We first brainstormed a list of criteria of what was most important to all. Next, we generated options and the group was able to gain greater clarity on what was important to them during the evaluation process: to select an option or to combine options that would help gain the most benefits while mitigating drawbacks.

Business S.O.S. can create the best organization design, yet it takes not only people but also the *right* people to make it effective. Therefore, special care needs to be taken in determining the hiring and training process when it is required. There are two things to keep in mind when filling these roles:

1. Fill the most senior open roles first.
2. Many of these roles will be drastically different than they were before, due to the impact of IT and globalization. The task of hiring qualified human resources within budget constraints will ensure that you have the right fit of talent and that incumbents clearly understand they have a new role.

Business S.O.S.™

Plan for implementation, paying close attention to the people issues involved. A big change requires a great deal of detailed planning to make it effective. Consider pacing (going neither too fast or too slow), sequencing of changes, pilot efforts, and communication in your plans. Additionally, ensure that your plans involve alignment of people-practices to the new organization, such as union renegotiations, compensation issues, training needs, and performance measures. Many redesign efforts neglect this last point and then find themselves with a wonderful design that isn't realized in day-to-day practices.

The Business S.O.S. Website

Though there are many business coaches, mentors and professionals who offer help to reorganize and reconstitute these distressed businesses, these primarily belong to the unorganized sector. They are disbursed throughout the country and there exists no single private sector organization that brings these mentors and distressed businesses together. This is where Business S.O.S. comes into the picture. The whole idea is conceived to address this need of bringing together distressed businesses and business service providers, helpers and volunteers to revive these distressed businesses using modern technology through proprietary software and the Internet.

In order to take this idea to a global platform, Business S.O.S. will establish a website that will be a global, online platform where distressed businesses, organizations and individuals seeking help can access and hire independent freelance coaches, mentors and professionals and use online collaboration tools to seek advice, coaching, mentoring, and any sort of help to bring their businesses out of distress.

The web portal serves the following objectives:

- To facilitate distressed businesses in finding suitable coaches mentors and professionals for help in various areas relating to operations, marketing, finance and even industry specialists.
- To facilitate professionals across the globe in finding suitable clients so that their skills can be used to grow and mutually develop business relationships.

Independent coaches, mentors and professionals would be able to create online profiles and portfolios, offer assistance, and collaborate and receive payment through the web portal.

Both distressed businesses and resource persons will be required to register on the website before they can access/offer services. This registration process will go through a robust validation process by Business S.O.S.. This validation process will not only stop spammers, but will also provide identify verification of all registrants. Two types of registration will be available on the website: free registration and premium registration.

The distressed business registrant will post it's needs and requirements on the website. Based on certain well built, backend calculations, matching resources and individuals, and/or groups, will be suggested to the distressed business. Similarly, alerts will be sent to the matching resource persons and/or groups. With free registration, the number of needs, requirements, and services applied for and posted by businesses and resource persons will be limited. The matching of the requirements and skills will be done by the Business S.O.S. website.

Apart from premium registration fees, Business S.O.S. will also build other revenue streams, such as member and non-member advertising, banners, TV shows, Radio shows, sale of books, templates, and applications, etc.

The website would be a fully interactive website, offering, among other services, self-help, group and individualized assistance, free information, individual and group training and webinars, and other resources, including live consultation and group assistance and forums.

The website would also be robust and embrace the latest technology, thereby enabling itself to be accessed from the latest PCs, tablets, smart phones and so on.

The idea of this website has been conceptualized based on the needs of distressed businesses. These distressed businesses cannot afford to have full time experts on their payroll to address various issues that arise from time to time. As and when there is a need for a specialist in any field of business, these businesses can simply log on to the web portal, post their requirements. The web portal will be smart enough to short list and suggest professionals from its database. The professionals can also apply to the business' requirements based on their skill sets.

Business S.O.S. ™ is conceived to address this need of bringing together distressed businesses and business service providers, helpers, and volunteers to revive these distressed businesses using modern technology and Internet.

The web portal would function both as a search engine and as well as a connecting link between the

Business S.O.S.™

distressed businesses and the professionals. The main functions of the portal involve the following:

- The portal would function as a bridging link between the distressed businesses and professionals offering to help these businesses by providing services of a specialized nature.
- The portal would act as a virtual meeting place for the businesses and professionals, which would include workrooms, chat rooms and also facilities for file sharing.
- The portal would be the one stop shop for all requirements of businesses including posting of requirements, short listing of professionals, portfolios, samples, ratings, feedback, history of work etc.
- The portal would also have facilities to generate reports on time taken, amount spent and so on, which would act as an information system for both the businesses and the professionals.
- The portal would have enhanced transparency from both sides whereby the businesses can monitor the professionals'

progress of work and the professionals would also have facility to monitor and track their payment status.

Bottom Line: Is Organizational Redesign a One-Time Thing?

A great leader is one who, when necessary, is willing to not only recreate his or her organization and entire approach to business but also to anticipate those changes. For many of us, we simply were not prepared for the financial meltdown that shocked the markets and destabilized many of our well-established business models. A true leader of a modern business needs to keep in mind that by the time changes are implemented, it may be time to change again. Under the adverse economic conditions we all live in, we can all grow from the fact that our business life cycles are now at a hyper accelerated pace.

The Business S.O.S. website (www.businesssos.com) is accessible for all to preview. All you need to do is register your firm with a special password, and immediately you will begin the process of evaluation by our team of experts. It would be impossible at the infancy stages of our concept to over-promise that we can completely change each and every company, all at once.

Business S.O.S.™

We need to build our network of trusted service and product providers as well as our volunteers and sponsors. But what we can promise is that each company will have access to a host of volunteers and resources that can be immediately utilized.

We will also be available by phone. Call us directly or contact us through your mobile device. We need to show our public officials that if small business employs over half of the work force in America, policies should be developed to level the playing field once again. The only way this can happen is through a collaborative effort.

Business S.O.S. in and of itself is a new creative business model. In order to truly embrace and desire to participate in the offerings of Business S.O.S., we need to establish trust. In the daily lives of our customers, employees, and ourselves, we view life through three screens, namely, Television, Internet, and Mobile Devices. Through these three screens, we will by communicating our methods and successes. You can see what we do through our extreme redesigns featured on TV and the Internet. These industry-specific *enter-training*™ shows will run as shorts on various daytime online networks. Our Internet service capability is digitally accessible 24/7. You can also receive our news alerts via social media and Business

S.O.S. apps. Through our concept of redesigning companies, we can hope to have companies that are increasingly productive and workers with jobs that pay better salaries. Business S.O.S. is your business tool to facilitate critical collaboration and interconnectivity. It is a 21st Century business model.

Chapter 4
Partnerships, Integration and a Collective Big Think!

Bernd Schmitt, in his book, *The Big Think Strategy: Leverage Bold Ideas and Leave Small Thinking Behind,* notes the irony that many business leaders and their organizations want big thinking, "but cannot produce it because their organizations are trapped in a mode of small thinking that kills creativity right from the start. This kind of 'Small Think' is characterized by inertia and resistance, narrow-mindedness, and risk aversion that stifle true innovation." Larger organizations will notice this in their functional silos that behave independently. "Small Think is what managers get paid to do."[1]

So, if the problem at companies with functional silos is lacking a sufficient view of the company's operations, then this problem also affects a company's leadership. By thinking big and formulating a collaborative effort to redesign our small businesses one company and community at a time, groups of companies can then pull ourselves from this yoke of survival mode--or worse, the panic of doing something else quickly. Leaders and their companies can make more connections, see a greater purpose, and move back into profitability. Not only does this rejuvenate the sheer joy of runny a business but we also through networks will be able to compete with our large business counter parts on the global stage and grow our GDP. Many have intuitively been adapting to this type of horizontal business model out of necessity.

Forms of Alignment

Once the "Big Think" dawns, leaders have three basic options: they can build the expertise or machinery or capacity needed; they can buy it (an outsource model); or they can ally with other companies. This alliance can take one of three basic forms: a strategic alliance, a joint venture, or a consortium. Legally nuancing these forms is beyond this book's scope. This chapter focuses on allying with other companies in some sort of partnership, meaning any of the three forms of alliance.

Each day we are asked to provide faster and more efficient services and product delivery. How can we possibly meet the demand before it is too late if we do not align with or trust in colleagues to help guide and gain traction? I have read countless articles about partnerships. Yet many of us simply do not have the confidence, knowledge, or skill set to find or forge profitable and non-litigious relationships at the speed it would be necessary in these troublesome times. Many of us simply have not developed this level of what I call "IT liquidity" or the complex network of relationships that make working with new unknown partners an easy model to follow.

Business S.O.S. will provide through its website and membership the ability to connect to a specific source/vendor/alliance or possible partner with the desirable assets to reinvigorate each business. We will also set in place a membership agreement that each category of member must sign off on in order to be part of this unique network of businesses. It is based on a commitment to establish the highest-level corporate governess and business ethics--values that should always be part of our American culture. I think it necessary to re-establish this in order to revivify this diminishing corporate culture. Our community is in crisis, and each member needs to provide the leadership and opportunity to trust others. By utilizing the Business S.O.S. infrastructure, individual companies will be allowed the resources to support one another in this community-based effort. In summary, we need to trust each other to effect the level of change we need at the fast pace we need it without looking over our shoulder.

Partnerships, Integration and a Collective Big Think!

Century of Partnerships

Most companies are unable to house all of the disciplines and resources, human or otherwise, in a single infrastructure. In our current climate, the primary reasons are mostly financially and competency driven. We simply do not have enough capital to develop our businesses or manage the rapid advances in technology as in the past when business strategies were developed vertically.

My agency housed all of the disciplines under one roof: strategic thinking, account service, creative direction, production, media buying, public relations, traffic, copy writing, web master, direct mail experts, and more. Today, I would not think of developing an infrastructure that large because of the overhead cost as well as the inefficient and slow rate of service delivery. IT now provides the ability to function with employees and executives working through cloud computing in one office or many locations. This is another example of how drastic in the short term IT has change how business services are managed and delivered.

A study by the London School of Economics--based on a survey of 1,035 businesses and IT executives--found that the cloud will have a strong near-term impact on the majority of organizations. Twenty percent of the respondents were already using cloud capabilities for a variety of services, including corporate email, websites, storage, and customer relationship management. Similar numbers plan to make the transition in the next 18 months, thus doubling cloud usage in a very short time. This flexibility is a positive outcome, but with these new advantages, the customer becomes increasingly demanding in their expectations. The result is adopting a 24/7 availability of secure and top quality, client service.

One executive interviewed, Wolfgang Feisst of SAP, emphasized, "Today we deliver a service that needs to run the first time on. That means that every hour, day-by-day we are faced with customer needs, and it means each vendor needs to deliver a very high level of service."[2]

These are the very type of changes and investments most small businesses find so daunting, Cloud computing, although offering a do-it-yourself capacity for business owners, results in many of those owners having to manage a more complex, hybrid environment. Once this environment was inside the company, but, now, it's outside the firm.

The skill to utilize this exterior environment to develop outsourced capabilities and grow your productivity is the quantum leaps so many of us are afraid to take. Most small business owners are control oriented. Changing this

Partnerships, Integration and a Collective Big Think!

strategy keeps costs down and communication up, but it requires a level of trust from business owners in these exterior source providers. By using Business S.O.S. and its committed culture of honesty and corporate governess, business owners will be able to create easy partnerships or alliances to acquire business capacities that each small business may be too small by itself to handle or expand market reach into a much broader trading area with even global potential. IT and now cloud computing are intuitively fostering professionals seeking quid-pro-quo relationships. Business S.O.S. will be the training ground.

      How will this network work? On the website Business S.O.S., members will each complete a questionnaire that documents their businesses. Answers will record, bit-by-bit, the complete DNA of each company. Again, these companies will range from concept to current distressed status. So different kinds of information needs to be collected from the rationale behind the name and its digital significance to the date of incorporation and the financial life cycles that each member business has encountered. What products or services does each provide? Is this business model still viable for the 21st Century? If so, then what are the myriad of resources it needs to get out of survival mode and back on track? Each resource

Partnerships, Integration and a Collective Big Think!

company is guided by its commitment to work with the highest level of ethics and corporate governess because many of our businesses and business owners are in a vulnerable state of distress. They need a significant level of comfort and reassurance when discussing the intimate details about their businesses.

Partnerships and alliances with key peoples and companies are crucial for small businesses to succeed. Good alliances help businesses tremendously to overcome competition. The key objectives of strategic business alliances are:

1. Innovating product or services
2. Entering new markets or reaching new customers
3. Increasing production and delivery capacity, while keeping inventory lean
4. Ensuring a least expensive supply of raw materials or resources
5. Increasing marketing share or outrunning competitors
6. Improving after-sale customer service

Partnerships, Integration and a Collective Big Think!

Strategic alliances can help a company provide security, software, technology, service, and consultation. The number of solid alliances they develop and maintain effects the growth phase of a modern day company.

How to Set Up a Strategic Alliance

Strategic alliances are sweeping through nearly every industry and are becoming an essential driver of potential growth. Alliances range in scope from an informal business relationship based on a simple contract to a joint venture agreement in which, for legal and tax purposes, either a corporation or partnership is set up to manage the alliance.[3]

For small businesses, strategic alliances are a way to work together with others toward a common goal while not losing their individuality. Alliances are a way of reaping the rewards of a team effort--and the gains from forming strategic alliances appear to be substantial. Companies participating in alliances report that as much as 18 percent of their revenues come from their alliances.

But, it isn't just profit that is motivating this increase in alliances. Other factors include an increasing intensity of competition, a growing need to operate on a global scale, a fast changing marketplace, and industry convergence in many markets (synergy between service and manufacturing companies are overlapping more and more in the products/services they supply). Especially in a time when growing international marketing is becoming the norm, these partnerships can leverage your growth through alliances with international partners. Business S.O.S. is here to make these transitions more automated and readily available to its members rather than take on the risk and expense. For example, one can enter international markets by finding an appropriate alliance with a business operating in the marketplace you desire to enter.

Business S.O.S. has been developed to be the catalyst to this type of team ventures and solutions. Because of the quantum changes discussed, we clearly see a trend to advocating our small businesses toward highly specialized niche markets by providing highly specialized products and services. We see where competition has fostered outsourcing of all but core capabilities and developed the right alliances enhances competitiveness, growth and cost efficiencies.

A *strategic alliance* is essentially a partnership in which you combine efforts in projects ranging from getting a better price for supplies by buying in bulk together to building a product together with each company providing

Partnerships, Integration and a Collective Big Think!

part of its production. The goal of alliances is to minimize risk while maximizing leverage and profit.³

Alliances are often confused with mergers, acquisitions, and outsourcing. While there are similarities in the circumstances in which a business might consider one of these solutions, they are far from the same. Mergers and acquisitions are permanent, structural changes in how the company exists. Outsourcing is simply a way of purchasing a functional service for the company.

An *alliance* is simply a business-to-business collaboration. Another term that is frequently used in conjunction with alliances is establishing a business network. Alliances are formed for joint marketing, joint sales or distribution, joint production, design collaboration, technology licensing, and research and development. Relationships can be vertical between a vendor and a customer, horizontal between vendors--local or global. In order to rapidly react to the current business climate and assist our companies, we will activate every potential source relationship for our members. The results are:

- Achieve advantages of scale, scope and speed
- Increase market penetration

- Enhance competitiveness in domestic and/or global markets
- Enhance product development
- Develop new business opportunities through new products and services
- Expand market development
- Increase exports
- Diversify
- Create new businesses
- Reduce costs.

Strategic alliances are becoming an increasingly more common tool for expanding the reach of your company without committing yourself to expensive internal expansions beyond your core business. We need to help each other develop the skill set to making team or business alliances work quickly and easily.

Growth of "teaming"

From the football field to the boardroom, a coordinated team effort is critical. The drive toward product or service differentiation has led firms to concentrate on niche markets and provide highly specialized services or products. In addition, competition has fostered outsourcing of all but the core capabilities of a firm. In this environment, *teaming*--firms seeking partners to provide commodities and services as needed. The growth in the size and complexity of our business environments has resulted in the necessity of a team effort.

Government Teaming: Remember the Department of Defense (DOD) Guidebook in Chapter 2? Its purpose was to assist small firms in successfully bidding on larger defense projects. It provided acquisition strategy teams with a road map on how a group of small businesses could meet the requirements. Although this strategy alone will not overcome every problem faced by small businesses, it does open the door by broadening competition on large DOD contracts. The guidebook also serves as a resource for acquisition strategy teams to help level the playing field for small businesses. It offers several examples of real--world strategies to encourage the participation of teams in DOD acquisitions.[4]

Even the language sounded familiar to that used by our initial strategy members. So, the government is well aware that there is not a level playing field for small businesses whether they are looking to bid on a government contract or they are competing with Wal-Mart in a local market. The acknowledgement confirms a problem exists for which they are trying to find a solution through the Small Business Administration. We need the government at all levels to help small businesses develop these teaming skills and initiatives. It does not have to be a strategy secretly utilized only for defense contracts but could also be an all-out effort to help bring small businesses out of survival mode and foster global business outreach of these businesses increasing our exports and initiate the U.S. leadership in global expansion.

Teaming Pros and Cons: Although teaming is a customary business strategy for most large businesses, many small firms often practice a go-it-alone strategy for a variety of reasons. For example, some small business owners do not want to give up control. Others avoid teaming because they want to have a direct relationship with the customer, and teaming (as a subcontractor) may mean either no relationship or minimal contact with the main customer. Still others fear investing in a proposal, only to be squeezed out by the prime contractor, who refuses to negotiate with a team member. Additional reasons include limited resources--for example, legal expertise--or prior negative teaming experiences.

Partnerships, Integration and a Collective Big Think!

Mergers and Acquisitions 3.0: Mergers and acquisitions (M&A) is another tool for modernizing business and your business skill set. An *acquisition* is when one company absorbs another, usually through some combination of cash and stock and assumes all the assets and all the liabilities of acquired firm. A *merger,* in contrast, is when two firms are worth more together than they were apart. By joining forces, they could start a positive financial strategy and experience a quick turnaround for growth and profitability.

Either approach could speed up the growth process for many small businesses that do not have the time to do market research and lay the groundwork for expanding in new or global markets. Matching firms who would benefit from an M&A takes patience and trust.

At Business S.O.S., our teams will watch for these prime growth opportunities for companies to join forces. Along with providing critical speed to the growth process M&A is a great strategy to assemble the kind of talent necessary to meet a larger market's demand. Most owners seek out the sort of company management to expand their businesses. If talent is promoted to stay on after the M&A, it also allows companies to buy knowledge that sometimes takes years to acquire. M&A's are another way to enter new markets in a connected world. To think and grow in this new business climate, we have to adapt to a new way of thinking about our business models and life cycles. It is no longer about creating a company and expecting that company to function the same in the next 5 years as it did in the previous 5 years. We need to erase our boundaries and borders, and collaborate at a more rapid pace to join forces with our business colleagues.

    Business S.O.S. wants to create a culture in which competitors need not be bitter rivals, but view each other as possible collaborators at the right moment of growth or stagnation. This is what our large business counterparts have known and done for years. M&A can and will be part of the solution for many of our struggling companies. For example, picture a business that has been in survival mode for four years. This strategy could realize economic gains, such as economies of scale, combining complementary resources, garnering tax advantages, and eliminating inefficiencies. Other reasons for considering growth through an acquisition include property rights to products or services, increasing market power and brand awareness, penetrating new geographic regions, and providing management with new opportunities for growth and advancement at a faster pace.

Partnerships, Integration and a Collective Big Think!

"In today's global business environment, companies may have to grow to survive, and one of the best ways to grow is by merging with another company or acquiring other companies," said business consultant Jaclyn Sherriton in an interview with *Entrepreneur Magazine*. "Massive multi-billion dollar corporations are becoming the norm, leaving an entrepreneur to wonder whether a merger ought to be in his or her plans as well", Sherriton continued.[5]

Without solid ethical resources in M&A, Business S.O.S. would not have a complete compliment of offerings to the 21st Century entrepreneur. We need to make these resources easily evaluated by our members, affordable and delivered by a group of ethical volunteers and professionals.

Promoting and providing the entire suit of offerings to businesses which includes partnerships, alliances, teaming and mergers will afford many small businesses the opportunity to survive and thrive in these continued dysfunctional economic times.

Chapter 5
Activism: Your Most Authentic and Effective Marketing Tool for the 21st Century

Senator John McCain, the Republican presidential nominee in 2008, remarked concerning the flow of money into lobbying and election campaigns as "nothing less than an elaborate influence-peddling scheme in which both parties conspire to stay in office by selling the country to the highest bidder."[1]

Business S.O.S. was conceived not only out of my own suffering and perceived failures but also a firm commitment to embrace this extraordinary moment and take action to enhance my own financial position and that of others. Many of us have had to fend off not one financial calamity within a decade, but five significant blows--each shattering my stability and that of millions of entrepreneurs across a broad spectrum of industries.

I have alluded to the emotional pain it encompasses to go from success and security to instability, confusion, and despair. In my journey, I was fortunate enough to have taken this unimaginable set of circumstances as an invitation to expose myself to all of the research and information that has now begun to accumulate. I am

Activism: Your Most Authentic and Effective Marketing Tool for the 21st Century

learning about the dysfunction of our financial and political institutions. This feat may be accomplished by embracing what I believe is the cultural imperative of our time: to become a new age American Patriot and establish a viable solution that will provide a platform for me and other entrepreneurs to find an earnest, proactive alignment of our responsibility as citizens in trying to collectively correct this plight that imperils all of us.

Chapter 1 addressed our two functioning economies, namely, the global trade economy of large, multi-national companies often whose stock is traded on Wall Street; and the rest of us 99 percenters (25.4 million registered companies in the U.S.) whose focus is Main Street. We have an economy experiencing solid growth for the top 1 percent coupled with the other more stagnant economy for the 99 percenter.[2] We have proof that the growth for the top 1 percent of companies and their CEOs--Wall Street, "too-big-to-fail" banking institutions, pharmaceutical and health care firms, and oil companies with access to "rents" and government subsidies--have enjoyed a greater share of the nation's income than previous generations. Meanwhile, the rest of us continue to experience a state of survival, stagnation, and threat that we may not be able to pull ourselves out of this mess if it lasts any longer.

When economics became political, large corporations increased their vast power to influence policy and laws. This benefited them, but shattered the underpinning of our great society. Hedrick Smith--a Pulitzer Prize-winning journalist--wrote *Who Stole the American Dream?* This comprehensive piece of journalism outlines, in detail, how laws and policies lobbied by our large financial institutions have stacked the deck against America's small businesses and working class. They also enticed millions into subprime mortgages and inadequate 401k retirement packages. The result? Hope or possibility of retirement for millions of our citizens swept away. In effect, this has eliminated the dream of retiring with dignity. Yet the payday for top tier executives has created the greatest disparity in incomes, out-flanking even the Gilded Age.[3] Washington is in complete lock-step with the power and might of our financial institutions and big corporations. Senator McCain got it right.

In my microcosm, the soul of this nation is not oblivious to the indiscretions of our political leaders and our out-sized institutions. Republican or Democrat, we all know that we have serious and far-reaching structural problems exacerbated by political shenanigans. Do politicians really believe we do not know what they are up to? People talk about it openly. Mr. Smith asks when is the underbelly of citizens going to say, "Enough is enough?" When will we venture out in the street and demand the kind of changes that fueled the grassroots efforts of the Civil Rights Movement, the environmental movement, the labor movement, and the women's movement? He says *citizen power* won important political victories that altered the face of our society and enlarged the American dream. When there are insiders with extra power and clout, our democracy becomes unfair and unequal. Smith calls his book a CAT scan of the two Americas: these "polarizing political theatrical performances reinforce economic inequality and along with it, a pervasive sense of economic insecurity."[4]

    He reconfirms, along with other economists, that we are in the throes of enormous structural changes that cannot be solved as in decades past.[5] I am encouraged by the recent focus by journalist to sleuth this inadequately reported cataclysm so many of us now face. Most of us have been fighting our own fiscal cliffs for over five years. It is about time more of us recognize the need to not only organically spread the information but also to come up with viable action-driven solutions to get us out of this financial ditch into which we allowed our large corporate colleagues to drive us.

During the run up to the 2008 elections, I was being courted by all of the Democratic nominees. They assumed just like me that I was still affluent and influential. I still did not realize my own corporate health was on life support. I had already heard the heart monitor's warnings that would eventually unravel my firm. I remember meeting then-Senator Joe Biden in a small intimate gathering during the time he was a presidential candidate. He asked me personally why I was endorsing Barak Obama. I can remember how President Kennedy demonstrated greatness when he crystallized and elevated his new presidency with his "ask not what your country can do for you" moment. It brought the nation forward toward a common goal as a force of good in the world. I told Senator Biden that many Americans were hoping Obama would send a similar galvanizing message. . Historians will judge Obama's presidency and whether or not it has obtained significant achievements despite the gridlock of Congress. The damage Congress inflicted by the downgrade of America's credit rating from AAA status will be felt for many decades to come and it was indicative of the partisan politics that has marred this administration. Control of power and money is more important than the public good in Washington. This attitude by both political parties may have pleased their bases, but it did not ensure the Republicans the White House in 2012 or a popular vote or Electoral College victory. In 2014 it may result in many surprises for the Democrats in the Senate and Congress as well as they are also willing participants in this unholy marriage between themselves and special interest groups.

      Despite being satisfied with the passing of the Lilly Ledbetter Fair Pay Act for women and the repeal of the "don't ask, don't tell" policy, I was disappointed that President Obama did not accomplish more in his first term. Health care is a basic human right, and we are behind other advanced nations in figuring out how to deliver affordable healthcare for our citizens whether or not they had pre-existing conditions. Is that not when you need adequate health care the most? But there were several times I thought President Obama stayed silent when it was an opportunity to show his greatness. One of these instances was during the oil spill in the Gulf. This incident could have been the lightening rod to jolt the US to be a leader in all forms of sustainable energy. He could have used the spill as a bully pulpit to educate and lead the world in climate change and energy, yet he inexplicably remained silent.

This new gold rush (sustainable energy) would have energized the US market, as well as the world, in focusing on innovation in sustainable options in manufacturing and production, vast R&D projects, and more. During the dot.com era, I had obtained two significant universal resource locators (URLs), and their revenue added over $24 million to my gross bottom line. If the president had launched an all-out renewable focus, all I would have needed was one small company to resuscitate my business to the level it once was. This is an example of how government can step in and focus the country and entrepreneurs can benefit.

There also was no real policy to address the state of small business. "Jobs, jobs, jobs" was the rhetoric of Obama's campaign, but naturally Congress was not about helping him help thousands of individuals receive any more subsidies in this regard. So here, we are five years after the Great Recession and 99 percent of us are still vulnerable to the next crisis.

One of the most profound and disturbing observations reported by Hedrick Smith is the philosophical shift of America's business leaders from an inclusive style of leadership from 1940s to 1970s (that shared the nation's gains widely with the middle class) into a more self-centered style of leadership from the 1980s onward (that kept most of the economic gains at the top of the economic ladder). He quotes Arnold Toynbee's analysis: such a shift may reflect a time in a civilization when the political and business leadership class changes from acting as a "creative minority" (that inspires and leads the rise and flowering of a civilization) into becoming the "dominant minority" of "exploiters" (that is focused primarily on sustaining and expanding their own wealth and power).[6] This shift in the mindset of the elite is a major cause of the schisms of society and politics that contribute to the disintegration of a civilization.

President Obama is currently holding all of the cards. The Bush tax cuts expired at the end of the 2012. I believe to the majority who voted in favor of his re-election he had an obligation to hear our mandate to let these expire for the top 2 percent of earners.[7] For middle class and individuals earning $250,000 or less, a sustained tax cut or sustained payroll tax holiday is acceptable. To continue this tax cut on the backs of middle class families would not favor his legacy. Here is another moment to show greatness by not punishing the top 5 percent but engaging them in economic patriotism and utilizing this as the catalyst to ignite a movement that could bring America back for the benefit of all, and not just a few. Here again he remained silent.

I believe I am not the only one that sensed the greatness that lies in President Obama. He has won the electorate by a significant majority that I believe accepted his argument that it was impossible to fix the economy within this time frame when it took three or four decades to destroy it. But now many others and I will judge President Obama against the one issue that is at the core of our now-fragile democracy and that surrounds the statement by Senator John McCain. The corruption of our political process will define President Obama's legacy. For just as he could have captured the moment during the Gulf oil spill, he must rise to the moment and accomplish overriding and significant campaign finance reform before it is too late. We have given him the power to do it. As of this writing I believe he will not buck his own political party by endangering their hold on the powers that corrupt this entire political system and thus the environment small businesses operate.

The sheer radical nature of the Supreme Court to confirm Citizen United into law is an example of how anything goes as long as it is straight down party lines.[8] This ruling exhibits a degree of cynicism that the American public does not recognize the free reign that has been given to big businesses once again to change the course of a presidential election by buying and influencing votes. This is a dramatic assault against individual Americans--where each vote should count equally--rich or poor, black or white, gay or straight. As we all watched and wondered if a few billionaires could overtly buy the election, I heard a sense of relief. It did not work this time but it very well could in a future election. Here again, allowing big business the chance to perpetuate an already unfair playing field and promoting the chance to even lower taxes for millionaires and billionaires once again.

Another failure of Obama's first term was a complete lack of accountability of our "too big to fail" banking institutions. In case after case there was a pattern of fraud, deception, or violations of securities laws--but not once did the Justice Department intervene. Despite the near collapse of our entire economy, and with so many Americans destroyed in the aftermath, these big banks and their executives only received modest fines and settlements. With sub-prime mortgages, derivatives, and predatory loans our economy remains dysfunctional. This continues to hurt the average American and the health of small businesses with their need to capitalize and reinvigorate. With his new mandate, President Obama needs to enact effective regulatory reform. Here again is the power of special interest above the rescue of average Americans. It is regulations for small companies and no regulations for large firms.

    I scanned a few of my tax returns from the late 1990s. I was paying the Clinton era tax rate of 35 percent.[9] I believe I paid in those days $1.3 million to $1.7 million in federal income tax. During that time, I was so busy enjoying the creative aspects of growing my own business that I was in shock it was such a large amount. I knew I was doing well, but not that well. Guess what? I was happy to pay--it meant I was making money. Not only that, I had a tremendous sense of my civic responsibility to pay back this great country that was allowing me to follow my dream of becoming a self-made millionaire and develop an illustrious career in the once-respected advertising sector. This was a true accomplishment for someone like me who grew up in a traditional Italian home where women were teachers or social workers. Progress: I was living the American Dream.

Activism: Your Most Authentic Tool

This Crisis Can Open Doors that We Never Saw or Imagined

After enriching my knowledge and coming to terms with the true state of our republic, I was amazed that there were not more active movements reacting to this constant assault from this gaping disparity and dysfunction of our economic and political systems. How could I be the only one outraged in the small business community? Then I began to remember the stages I went through before I arrived at this enlightened moment.

I mentioned in Chapter 3, that, at first, there were months of denial where I simply couldn't fathom that I was not able to entice or close business deals as usual. I believed it would change. Then a strange tiredness, malaise, or listlessness set in where I just did not have the same passion or drive that was the keynote of my earlier success. After this continued, I became shocked at my reality and the prospect that not just me, but the whole economy was going down the tube. Once I became fully cognizant of all the mitigating reasons why we were all short-changed, I became angry. Now after five long years, I realize that the key missing ingredient to changing my trajectory was to build resilience and redefine all of my skills for marketing, media, complex strategic planning and thinking, as well as an innate desire to make a difference and view myself in an

Business S.O.S.™

activist role. After all those years of creating memorable fashion campaigns for luxury brands--although creatively challenging--it never brought me the kind of self-satisfaction with which a career of my caliber should culminate. By employing resiliency, I could make this experience an opportunity for professional and personal growth.

For many years, I worked with governmental institutions and developed complex, strategic marketing programs with thousands of participants. I had already begun to retool my traditional advertising and branding agency DJS Marketing to DJS 3SOP (Three Screens-Zero Paper). After all, the impact of paper production on the environment is vast. I did not want to continue in something that lacked integrity. With my anger giving way to my natural instinct to win, I realized if I could completely retool and restructure my firm for 21st Century technology and global reach, so can many other firms.

Brought forth from my long history and expertise in all forms of media and branding, and my desire to add depth to my next entrepreneurial venture in the way of activism, Business S.O.S. was born. I needed a multi-media platform within my scope of expertise to assist me in reaching other distressed firms--hence, Business S.O.S.

Activism: Your Most Authentic Tool

This is a project I have now been developing for the past 18 months.

Business S.O.S. has a Civic Commitment

Many would agree: There is nothing worse than health problems. The next worse experience, then, is business failure. This book focuses on the loss of a business that you put your blood, sweat, and tears into--for some of us, this dedication has persisted for over twenty years. I have chronicled the rapid fall of my business because I felt it important that the reader or member of Business S.O.S. know I developed this concept because I had nowhere to turn for help. I believe at least one in three businesses could be saved from closure or bankruptcy with an intense experienced team of professionals who are willing to help our business owners put up a good fight.[10]

Yes, I have experienced failure first hand, and it is very painful. When I realized there was no real help that is when the concept of Business S.O.S. began to take form. It takes a certain amount of independence to want to start a company. This self reliance is a good thing in the beginning but can become a liability, first, by not developing close friendships with peers, and second, by honoring the taboo to talk about major business problems. According to recent statistics, 50 percent of small businesses fail within the first five years.[9] But, this rate has steadily increased to 85 percent--a staggering figure when this is supposed to be the land of opportunity.[11] Please see the chart in Chapter 1 for more information.

This illustration from Chapter 1 shows the changes from 2005 through 2011 with the number of new business starts falling nearly by half, closures increasing over two-fold, and bankruptcies increasing more than three times.

Gaining the Psychological Tools Toward Success

The moment we accept, as entrepreneurs, that a long stretch of survival mode or "going it alone" will not help us revitalize our businesses, we can develop the skills and tools needed to rebuild and redesign our businesses for the future. But, what happens if you do not come forward or act to work together with your neighbors? You suffer with negativity, worry, and even depression. After sacrificing so much of your capital in time and money, accepting the status quo can be stressful. It affects your life in every aspect: personal, professional, and financial. Frankly, I am sick of hearing the sad, terrible stories I hear every day and feeling powerless to help.

Activism: Your Most Authentic Tool

Yet, our hardship is part of the journey. I know I have carried this view. If I had not experienced such "highs" when my business was successful or such lows when the economy collapsed, I would not have gained the knowledge and direction toward reaching any new goals I have decided to pursue in the future.

In the past four years, I have read and studied a vast amount of literature on the economy, business methodologies, globalization, taxation, technology, financial instruments, finance, debt, bankruptcy law, social media, mobile marketing, and more. I see my failures at not understanding the market as a lesson in the life cycles of all businesses. What worked in 1990 surely could not work after the financial collapse of our markets in 2008. With IT, these businesses cycles will occur more often and at a rapid pace. Far more accelerated then companies have ever experienced change before in our most recent history. Hence, the value of my experience has cast me in the desirable position to ignite what I believe is the beginning of a much stronger movement to take our country back from anything too big. Seeing and having the chance to intensively evaluate my microcosm along with millions of other small businesses has been an opportunity for growth and learning. We can all take what is a negative situation and work together to turn this around by helping each other, which in turn will help ourselves rewrite this gap in fairness.

Some might object. It is true: We cannot expect to dissolve, for example, Wal-Mart, so that we have less retail competition. But, we can think of new innovative products, services, and marketing to compete with them locally and globally. We can better utilize the greatest communication tool developed since the printing press--the World Wide Web--and harness the fact that many new business models will wrap their product development around this information highway. We can also see and develop new ways of analyzing the new American role in the global marketplace and open up to new cultures and methods to deliver products and services globally. We need to change our perception and perspective all at the same time in order to get our confidence and excitement back for our businesses, our communities, and our country. We can now move forward with confidence because through Business S.O.S. you are not alone.

Our businesses are in tatters because of the shift in business practices created by big business and special interests. It is imperative that all small businesses-- including the ones that need help in their business redesign to the ones that will sponsor and volunteer--need to ignite and unite our capabilities and resources to quickly respond to those in need. This is our short-term goal, but it also establishes what our long-term programs will encompass and look like. It would be modeled just like any other civic call to action in times of need. Help is on the way. Activism will be an integral part of the new business culture in America.

Chapter 6
How to Keep Up with New Marketing Methods and Social Media

There is much to be discussed that is negative but there are also areas of opportunity that many small businesses have not been able to take advantage of due to the complexity of modern multimedia and the interface of the social networks. Never before in the history of small business is there a more cost effective way to communicate and seek new customers from all over the world. Marketing is the most important tool to let people know you are out there but it has radically changed since 2008. This is why I retooled my traditional marketing firm, which emphasized TV, direct mail and print media to one that is focused on three screens zero paper.

When I mention social media to small business owners, many freeze. When I ask them about their reaction, they point to the potential for time and energy drain, especially the complexity of learning and keeping up. Some even think that having a presence might expose their businesses to complaints or negative reviews. While these points have some validity, I think the opportunity far outweighs them. Never before, in the history of small

How to Keep Up With New Marketing Methods and Social Media

business, has there been a more cost effective way to communicate and seek new customers from all over the world.

Marketing as Social

Marketing is often defined in different ways. A social view of marketing would include selecting groups with needs and serve these at a sufficient price or return. This social view would also include promoting goods and services to people who can be reached in similar ways.

How such promotion operates, however, has radically changed since 2008. This is why I retooled my traditional marketing firm, which emphasized TV and print media to one that is focused on three screens zero paper. This is why many small business owners are *overwhelmed*. I have shared social media opportunities with many companies (including many well-known brands). Most small businesses are aware of marketing online and mobile devices, but few had a complete grasp of how to optimize these resources to meet their sales and marketing goals and objectives. Only a few more understood how to brand their products or services effectively.

More than a few have invoked the image of balls bouncing. They catch one and toss it into the air only to have ten more thrown their way. Because the options are so many, it is unclear which ones are right for them. In reviewing media plans and creative content, it becomes clear that many are guessing. The ability to learn quickly and develop a first class multimedia program for most small businesses is the daunting challenge. The first step in meeting this challenge is to assemble a database of options with descriptions of what exactly each can do.

The Business S.O.S. website will categorize thousands of marketing firms from the newest methods of creating creative campaigns to developing compelling content so important for the authenticity of enticing campaigns that are highly targeted and meaningful to bottom line sales. Business S.O.S. will have the online tools to help small and mid-size companies develop multimedia programs in a variety of categories and business sectors that have the analytics to interpret results.

Advertising and Branding, "Mad Men"-Style

Advertising and branding are something about which I used to know a lot after over 20 years in the business generating gross revenue of more than $25M per year providing a complete suite of offerings from branding, strategic creative and media plans as most full service agencies did at the time. The traditional campaigns we formulated for our clients were highly successful, and the creative and the media buys drove a positive response beyond what was measurable. Now not only is marketing much more complicated but also the selling of marketing by an agency is even more so because of these quantum changes in how to reach and communicate with current and new consumers. I believe most small businesses find the challenge of keeping up almost impossible.

Those over 30 years of age know the history of advertising. For those who are younger, watch Don Drapper in the series "Mad Men" to get a glance on what advertising and branding once was: great creative campaigns on a limited media menu. This included TV, radio, print ads in newsprint or magazines, direct mail, outdoor billboards, specialty items (such as T-shirts, hats, or pens) and third party endorsement through traditional public relations agencies.

When clients were pursued for a business partnership, they were pitched with storyboards, demo reels, or comprehensive layouts or dummy layouts ("comps"). Everyone assumed that if you were invited to respond to a request for proposal (RFP), a client was ready and willing to hire you based on the creative package you presented. There was a real respect for the intellectual property rights of the creative agency as well as the rights of the client who purchased these conceptions. Agencies like mine charged a premium for this type of strategic capability. Brands were "made" based on the visuals, copy, and tag lines as well as music ("jingles") and media placement associated with their products.

Some of the most memorable ad campaigns utilizing the criteria of the last four decades are remembered because of their impact on the growth of their brand and because they managed to hit on some universal truth that allows many of us to relate to and remember these campaigns years after they ran.

- Campaigns, like "Think Small" for Volkswagen, played right into the hands of its audience expectations. "You think I am small? Yeah, I am." They never tried to be something they were not.
- Miller Lite went after real men to sell low-calorie beer. There campaign featured two opposing groups often yelling either "Great

Taste" or "Less Filling." By breaking the assumptions (good tasting beer is high in calories; light or low calorie beer never satisfies), allowed Miller Lite to dominate the market for years.

- Nike's "Just Do It" appealed to that drive into which we all must tap in order to push further then we thought we could. This campaign connected to consumers at an emotional level and brought Nike sales in 1988 from $800 million to 1998 sales of $9.2 billion.

- There are the Absolute Vodka ads titled "The Absolute Bottle" which is the longest running ad campaign in history lasting over 25 years.

- Marlboro creating a lifestyle identity so memorable that we can all see images of this campaign even though they have not run on TV for years.

- There are many more such as Clairol's "Does She or Doesn't She?" "Got Milk" for California Milk Producers; Wendy's "Where's the Beef?" to name a few.

- My firm did a lot of fine jewelry and watch marketing, but the greatest and most successful jewelry campaign was for DeBeers: "A diamond is forever." *AdAge* declaring it the most memorable slogan of the 20th Century.

Many of these campaigns launched on TV or in print. These campaigns were produced for large global companies with enormous budgets, but they have one method in common, they all had great creative strategies and the right media mix.

This type of creative-focused marketing was emulated by smaller agencies like mine and was easy to execute in local or regional markets using similar creative methods and media strategies. Plenty of research tools were available to find out exactly where these campaigns ran. Then the media were so identifiable, we could just ask the media. Indeed, we could simulate this kind of program with smaller budgets, and they would be very effective.

Great creative and a high quality production capability were my hallmark. With all of my staff, vendors, and clients, it became a mantra to adhere to "DJS Quality" standards. We guaranteed our work to our clients, unlike other agencies. For them, if the client signed off and an error was discovered, the client was forced to accept the mistake. This never happened in my offices because of the guarantee I placed in all my client contracts. It is part of what made my firm so successful. The trust my clients each felt from all of our work was legendary in the luxury sector. This was the era in which I grew my business from living room cold calls to a multi-million dollar international firm specializing in the luxury sector.

When I started my business this respect for the creative process and intellectual property was part of business as usual. When I began my firm the Internet and desktop publishing were just coming into play; it was a major missed opportunity that I did not foresee its impact. My business could have become a digital agency in at least the late 1990s. But so many of us can get caught in looking back; until we reach the pinnacle of regret, learn from the past, and force ourselves to look forward will we realize that in today's business market place, speed and flexibility are paramount to all business models. These lessons many of us have learned the hard way, and they will not be forgotten so quickly.

Advertising and Branding Today

Business S.O.S.™

As we look and evaluate contemporized sales and marketing many of the campaigns do not have the same top of mind awareness because they are targeted to focused audiences and launched on specific social networks. The former way carpet-bombed the landscape; the new approach sets up IEDs. The former way used a cannon; the new approach uses a sniper's rifle. For the most sophisticated marketers and advertising agency, this change requires a sea change to a specialized skill set.[1]

If we juxtaposed the great campaigns of 2012, only some of us may have seen or be aware of some of them. Most of us, however, would not have even been exposed to their messaging because (1) these campaigns are more highly targeted; (2) they were activated on social media; and (3) they did not reach the general consumer as did broad national TV or print media buys did in the past.

- For example, The Guardian had the "Three Little Pigs" which focused on the value proposition of the news organization.
- Red Bull sponsored content across a multitude of digital outlets when it showed Felix Baumgartner's jump to earth.
- Oreo cookies celebrated its 100th

anniversary by an interactive campaign called "The Daily Twist" to the Oreo cookie.

Not only are these campaigns difficult to emulate creatively but also they are difficult to copy in terms of social media exposure or strategy. For a small business the budgets are not there for developing fully paid content as long as an hour or thirty minutes. They would never be able to reduplicate the depth of exposure online. We all want to produce memorable campaigns for our small companies, but the complete understanding by clients to be able to coordinate all of the components of all of their options and sell this effectively is very difficult. It takes state of the art equipment, quality IT service providers and sophisticated management systems even for small firms along with a comprehensive understanding of the latest methods in marketing specific products across channels.

When I retooled my traditional agency from DJS Marketing to DJS 3S0P (three screens zero paper) in 2009, most of my clients (past and new) did not fully understand what I was talking about. Even today, I go on all three screens for most new clients and few have their digital marketing properly scaled to the size of a computer screen, smart phone, or other mobile devices. I saw a gap in the market, and this is where my opportunity emerged. Clients at the small business level, however, are usually working with so many resources for their marketing needs that they cannot keep track or formulate a comprehensive branded look or campaign. Hence, when in doubt many simply spend the minimum. This makes getting out of the survival mode even harder because the minimum acquires few new and loyal customers. This mess of options and the need to apply way more time on marketing and sales and even "integrate marketing" into the product development--these are a large part of what is making running and succeeding in a small business today so difficult.

  The Business S.O.S. website is going to entice marketing members and resources that understand market niches and make sure the business owner is well schooled in the newest aspect of sales and marketing for their product category. Marketing in general will require much more of management time then ever before. Thank goodness for all the books--such as *Social Media for Dummies* (For Dummies Press, 2013; also in eBook format), and social marketing integration software, such as HubSpot.com--to make these efforts more doable by integrating understanding and operations into one system. What small business owners need is software that addresses a wider range of business functions, shows a fuller range of options, and is affordable to the smallest of business owners. This is the goal and objective of Business S.O.S.

There is also a tremendous amount of resistance to online marketing. Many clients speak of it with enthusiasm but to really get the needed authenticity of this type of communication, owners and key executives need to personally write or develop this content or find highly skilled motivated staff that will write it "like they would." For any small business owner who is based in reality he/she will know that they can start off strong but somehow I see millions of sites lying dormant. A website is a living and breathy entity and has to be nurtured and feed daily in order for it to be a usable and meaningful tool to enhance sales and provide optimal communication in a 24/7 top level service demand cycle.

I absolutely loved my business when I started and reached success within the expected five years of proving I could stay in business, increase sales, manage a professional staff and master all the financial aspect of running my business all the while setting my sights on growth. It had the perfect synergy of creativity that I loved as I acted as the key creative force in the agency although I employed high-level creative directors. I approved all campaigns before they were presented to clients. When the agency reached its zenith in 1999 I was focused on growing the business to $100M either by acquiring another agency or agencies or pitching larger accounts.

      This would have been a positive growth strategy, of course, if I had only retooled then to become a digital agency. This would have required me to re-train myself, and my key staff, to this revolutionary, digital movement before any crisis hit. And, the crisis did come shortly afterward in 2000 when we had the dot-com correction. This hurt my bottom line, and I started to make cut backs in areas that disabled my new focus. Like millions of other business owners, I did not have the academic training necessary; basically, I learned on the job, which worked when the business environment was fairly stable. The environment, looking back, was anything but stable. Many of us, aware of the boom-bust synergies' that our economy faces every few years, had no idea how bad things could get. The objective for all businesses in today's volatile economic climate is to have the speed and flexibility along with the supporting tools to weather any kind of these national or global storms. Business S.O.S. was conceived for this purpose.

      Retooling my firm was a challenge because I was late in the game and lost substantial capital. Finding the right human resources with the specific skill set to move forward was difficult enough. Then to guide them to create micro-designed campaigns with intimately written copy for the digital world at the quality I was used to delivering--this was not easy. Then I had to solicit clients utilizing these new tools and media without developing them in advance of acquiring the business. Clients were cash strapped and were willing to listen and learn but no one bought.

Birth of Business S.O.S. and Entertrainment™

When, in 2009, it became too difficult to convince clients that I had the answers for their marketing and business problems, I began to formulate the concept of Business S.O.S.--the perfect parallel to DJS 3S0P. Business S.O.S. is the development of a business model that is:

- fully integrated through a well-developed marketing strategy
- utilizes all the aspects of web 3.0
- has a highly targeted market base
- reaches these markets through all three screens in a compelling manner
- uses proprietary software.

Business S.O.S.™

Business S.O.S. is a one hour fully funded TV show or online show that *entertrains*™--it "entertains" while it "trains" its viewers. It will evolve into radio content, and publishing as a result of the completion of this book and then a handbook. It is a fully integrated website that

- fosters all the redesign components of the show
- through its memberships, and complex programming and software
- to match volunteers, sponsors, resources, and members to help each other crowd solve and retool many aspects of their businesses
- fulfills my need to pay forward for the coveted opportunity to utilize all of the skills that I developed in my past business model throughout my career
- recast these skills to become relevant in a new context through this multimedia program

Teaching the Resistance

When I pitched DJS 3S0P, everyone accepted an appointment with me. I had an excellent reputation in marketing, and they were in a need-to-know frame of mind. But no one bought like they did in the past because no one had the revenue to embark on new programs in sales and marketing. Meeting after meeting people took notes, pictures on their smart phones, and recorded what I said. Then they wanted to think about it.

It was then that I had a defining moment. I had to embrace what the market was telling me: I had become a teacher of marketing and business redevelopment. Business S.O.S. the website, this book, and all the components are a result of this Gestalt that the internet had created a different need and that I not only had to retool my entire office but my philosophy and corporate strategy. I (and this dynamic digital program) had to reject traditional sales and marketing methods-- withholding information as corporate secrets or property; treating marketing colleagues as competitors.

This type of corporate posturing was a thing of the past. Everyone is welcome to take part in all the offerings of Business S.O.S.. All of my competitors are now potential partners in pursuing and helping other small businesses. It is no longer business as usual. We want to entice as many high quality resources locally, regionally, nationally, and globally in order to make my members successful. This is the culmination of my transformation into a 21st Century digital agency. It is what I needed to do to re-tool my traditional agency DJS Marketing Group into DJS 3S0P and create my integrated benchmark of Business S.O.S..

The goal is to obtain millions of members, volunteers, sponsors and resources so that any business at anytime who finds they are in a tenuous lifecycle of their business can log onto Business S.O.S.™ to get the help they need when they need it the most. This crowd sourcing to problem-solving solution, in this type of climate, is revolutionary. And it's the only way I can see as an efficient, timely, and encompassing remedy for millions of business with limited capital, human resources, and know-how. This is trust at the highest level and hope for millions of businesses that are still in limbo after five long years of struggle.

Viral Video and Social Media

Online video is a way to engage your audience for far less money. The Internet is a publishing vehicle that has revolutionized the flow of written content (including pictures and graphics) for billions of users globally. Now we are seeing this includes the power of high definition

(HD), three-dimensional (3D) video. Viewing videos online is one of the fastest growing areas of content production and distribution. By its nature, well-produced video content is a faster and cheaper way to connect with consumers, making it a viable marketing option for small businesses.

In a recent article in the *Harvard Business Review*, Thales Teixeiria studies the impact of video content on viewers. He utilizes eye-tracking technology, facial expression analysis, and lab experiments to better understand why people are now choosing to view online videos and what features prompt viewers to share these videos with friends. In a recent article in the *Wall Street Journal,* Google's You Tube reported that more than one billion unique visitors watch more than six billion hours of You Tube videos a month.[1]

"History--from the transistor radio, then TV, from network to cable--tells us that advertisers follow the audience," says Mr. Efrati. He added that large advertisers, such as Proctor and Gamble, Kellogg, and Wal-Mart, will be buying ads along with family friendly videos or create videos themselves. The competition for these ads is now at play as Yahoo, Microsoft, AOL, Hulu, and others aim to offer more original content. Web video will continue to grow at an enormous rate, resulting in pressure on traditional media outlets. Small company marketers need to explore this media opportunity.[2]

There are new firms that specialize in the creation and distribution of this online video advertisement. Not only is the cost of such media placement far less expensive then network or cable buys but can also be 10 percent (or even one percent) of the costs of a traditional ad agency and paid mass media buys.

Lower cost is not the only reason to consider online video. Channel surfing, DVRs, and the growing use of second screens (smart phones and tablets), result in fewer people watching TV commercials than ever before. Who hasn't been frustrated at viewing up to 12 commercials running between show segments? This may be a cable company's attempt to solve local revenue problems now. But, they need to look ahead. This type of audience abuse will melt away as Internet or smart TV's become affordable and the content quality is enhanced on Internet outlets the consumer is going to happily make the switch. Already, Netflix videos can be streamed on digital devices.

This effective new tool is a conundrum for many small business owners as a new skill set needs to be adopted, quickly. Many owners are control freaks, and every aspect is reviewed as if it were an 8x10, flat, one-

Keeping Up With New Marketing Methods

dimensional advertisement. Video requires a unique skill to develop and, when clients are presented with a concept, they simply may not understand how to speak to their online viewer or they may not have the level of budget necessary to add "voice" or depth to this online buy. Video intimidates many small business owners at a time when they need to view it as a point of opportunity.

    The large global clients can hire the likes of Dream Works Animation; the small business owner has new companies. For example, Tongal.com features many multinational corporations as clients. Yet, its process is similar to Business S.O.S. in that both are online communities that connect businesses. Tongal.com is a four-year-old firm that for a fee, posts specs for projects and matches it with freelance creative talent willing to work for a relatively low fee. Say a company wants a 90 second video that mentions the brand twice and shows the logo for a second. Tongal.com members submit 250-word proposals that meet those specs and the brand company pays on average about $500 for the rights to the idea it likes the best.

    Many small businesses are unaware of these cost-effective resources to produce content. Business S.O.S. will make this type of information readily available as companies come online and become part of our network.

Business S.O.S.™

What if $500 for the idea seems too expensive for a small business? The advertisers can do it themselves, producing high quality content and effective distribution. These videos can be placed on their websites or posted on You-Tube.

"Why do this?", you might ask. Hubspot.com and others have characterized the sea-change in marketing as a shift from "outbound" to "inbound" in nature. Under the old "outbound" approach, companies bought ad space in newspapers, went to trade shows, phoned potential customers at dinnertime, and placed ads during appropriate shows or movies. We have purchased technologies such as caller id, TiVo, spam filters, and the like to escape from as much of this as we can.

"Inbound" marketing that is different than traditional outbound marketing. Companies develop attractive content that draws viewers to their websites and video postings. Businesses can use sophisticated hosting sites--Hubspot.com is an example--that use search engine optimization and sophisticated analytics to help clients understand how their content offerings draw viewers and which do not.

As ad viewership shifts online through video content, traditional measures of cost and effectiveness, such as cost per impression that dominate metrics for print, radio, and TV become less relevant. New ways of evaluating these videos and their viewers need to be established. Not only is the production of this type of video a new unique option for the small business but understanding its effectiveness and results can also encourage many small businesses to venture into the unknown. Over time, small companies will become an increasing part of this new vehicle to reach audiences in a larger trading area. Web video and novel distribution strategies are examples of the perfect opportunity to build a brand more rapidly while on a tight budget.

Mobile Smart Phones, Tablets, and Television

The rise in inbound video is just the warm-up. Across the news channels in the Spring of 2013 was the fact that "the average New Yorker is checking their cell phone 150 times a day." What does this Mobile migration mean for your business? Broad adaptation of the Internet, social media, and mobile devices has created a more sophisticated and less patient consumer. This demand by your customers, to deliver 24/7 availability with consistent quality and reliability, is of the utmost importance to each small business.

Gratification needs to be instantaneous for your customers--they want what they want, where and when they want it. These developments and the rapid and organic use of mobile devices represent the defining characteristic of your modern day consumer. Their needs serve as the driver of a mobile first approach to marketing.

This, however, creates the additional demand by the business owner to really engage these new marketing methods or simply become obsolete as a business. The obstacle for the entrepreneur is the overwhelming consumer data to analyze. Consumers expect a whole lot more out of brands--including personalized, on demand marketing and sales tools. There is a need for the always-on customer service capability. This has put a lot of pressure on small businesses to keep up with the pace and redefine their business strategy on a continual basis--these are always changing. Any gap between this consumer and product delivery perception must be viewed as a potential loss of business. Not only that but consumers also demand real and authentic exchanges.

I cannot tell you how many times I present this type of program to a client, and they express their integration into the social media as a variation of "Oh, yeah, I've seen that." Yet, they do not have the slightest idea that it involves them and their interface. Business owner: You cannot hire the right freelancer to be as personalized and authentic as you and your team. For this reason many businesses are falling flat.

A recent study confirms what I have been seeing on the ground. An EIU/Lyris survey, "Mind the Marketing Gap," notes:

> *When asked about the biggest obstacles to adopting a more effective digital marketing strategy, the executives surveyed cited the following as their top two: inadequate budgets for digital marketing and data base management (50 percent), and a lack of capacity for analyzing big data (45 percent).*[3]

When asked to enumerate, what are the largest drivers of change in the current marketing landscape, 58 percent noted that the digital environment requires much more speed and agility, while 50 percent admitted consumers are much more knowledgeable. It is clear from this study that the emerging problem for marketers in the digital space is they are having trouble harnessing the power of big data to meet and exceed the expectations of their increasingly savvy, target audience.

Rather than just being a consideration for your marketing budgets, the extent of Smartphone penetration has created a need for many companies to think mobile first across the whole organization. The average New Yorker statistic means there is a fundamental shift in how we are communicating with each other and more importantly how we are communicating and accessing information.

The path that leads people to your website has changed, and unless you have a clear strategy in place and a competent team you risk getting left behind. We almost saw this happen to the most savvy of large companies, like Facebook. It wasn't until they pivoted the entire company to be mobile first, that we're seeing their stock prices climb. While Facebook may be in a better position than most organizations to do this, now that the majority of users are accessing it via mobile devices, this must still apply to organizations across the board. Regardless of how online savvy you are, how mobile-centric you are, or where your point of conversion sits for your customers, the fact is that consumers are now mobile first, so you must be too. If you want to stand a chance of being relevant throughout this next digital shift, a fundamental change within your organization must take place.

Keeping Up With New Marketing Methods

The constant refreshing of your digital strategy across all three screens--Mobile, Internet, and TV--is key to your organizations success. So is it a case of whether your website works on mobile or whether your mobile strategy applies to your website. At Business S.O.S. we want to provide the understanding and the resources for small business to make these changes without fear or trepidation. Our resources will provide you with a solid understanding of the various mobile marketing strategies best suited for your category of business and match you to the resources that can apply these methods cost effectively. Business S.O.S. will provide access to the finest digital marketing firms in your city or region and provide daily up to date content to stay in front of the latest trends in digital marketing.

A Digital Institute will be part of Business S.O.S. online offerings. It will provide short courses to small business owners in need of basic or more formidable knowledge. Course topics ranging from simple message system (SMS) marketing, Mobile Internet, Mobile applications, mobile coupons, Bluetooth and proximity marketing, quick reference (QR) codes, emerging mobile technologies, where mobile fits in the marketing mix, and integration with traditional media.

Business S.O.S.™

Soon, the smart phone will house our whole life (if it doesn't already). I strongly suggest that small business owner's stop resisting what is inevitable and really learn to utilize and harness the power of mobile marketing.

Television's Screens are Dimmed until Smart TVs Dominate

According to the *Wall Street Journal,* broadcast television ratings have dropped sharply for the combined reasons of a continued weak economy and competition from other media. Web video outlets such as Hulu, Yahoo, Google, YouTube, AOL, Huffington Post, CN Entertainment, Weather Company, and Apple, are competing, head-to-head with advertising dollars. All analysts predict those sales will be flat or fall, up to 2.5 percent.[4]

Even print media giants like *Conde Nast* and the *Wall Street Journal* exhibited their video content strategy at the "Newfronts" that preceded the original "up-fronts." These media giants see the trends in video content and are trying to recast themselves as mini-TV studios. Will it work for them while the market is wide open for new players? For 100-year-old magazine conglomerates, they may find themselves in the same spot as their small business counterparts when they ask the likes of Anna Wintour and Brandon Carter to embrace this new video platform. This start-up is called CN Entertainment. They will be making overtures to old and new advertisers promising them intense marketing efforts in order to make sure people know the videos are out there.[5]

The *Wall Street Journal* is also in the video content game under the title of "WSJ Everywhere." Unlike *Conde Nast*, which hired an A-Team list of TV producers, the WSJ relied on their team of reporters to produce content in a makeshift studio. The results have been plenty of video, but a mixed bag in terms of quality. The *Journal* also announced a new documentary series, "WSJ Start Up of the Year," and lifestyle videos called, "WSJ Café." Like many of us these mature brands need to diversify because their legacy print product is declining at a rapid pace. Not only do these print giants want to compete with TV Networks but also with ad agencies as well. It has become a one-stop shop for marketers. This is the very beginning of all of this video production.

Apple TV is still testing designs for large screen HD sets. This will intensify the competition from Google and Samsung. After Apple makes its way into consumer living rooms and all the capability to integrate phones, laptops, and other mobile devices, it will entrench digital users viewing Internet video, content from AppleTV, Hulu, and Netflix. This will again create a massive shift in digital strategies. The U.S is the slowest market in growth of smart TV's because of cable companies' powerful grip on the viewer access. But, it will come just the same, and large cable companies like Comcast and Time Warner will have their own challenges in keeping up with technology.

One of the most dynamic opportunities in television today is branded content. Instead of having sponsored stories published on existing platforms, many brands are creating their own content and producing it with high quality material aimed at specific audiences. After retooling, I began developing branding campaigns utilizing this new media model.

"The new content model represents a shift in the way TV and publishing has usually worked. Rather than pay a media middleman for eyeballs, brands including Tory Burch, Coca-Cola and Gilt Groupe are learning to attract them all on their own. Instead of paying money to rent an audience," said John Hazard, director of Community for Content.[6]

As viewers stop watching traditional commercials, marketers have found new ways to keep them from tuning out. These new offerings, the marketers hope, will be entertaining enough to endear viewers to the brands behind them. Burger King is making a feature film the "King" character of its ad campaign. Office Max recently created a show on ABC Family. Anheuser-Busch plans to start a seven-channel TV network online, called Bud TV.

Smart TV sales have accelerated marketers to look to a whole new world. Consumers increasingly bypass commercials using digital video recorders, such as TiVo, and spend more time flipping through a wide array of television networks. This will continue to degenerate with Smart TVs providing the added distraction for viewers to check Emails, work a little, and catch other online videos. Business S.O.S. - The Show, its content is produced, specifically, to entertrain our markets along with a strategic plan to keep these consumers in bound and seeking to connect with all of our offerings.

Three Screens - Zero Paper

As with the rest of this book, I did not want the marketing chapter to become a tutorial on marketing. Rather, small business owners and staff need to see the big picture as to what has happened, where we are now, and what appears to be on the horizon. The Business S.O.S.^{TM}

website will rank and house all of the top resources available to receive and stay current on this rapidly changing environment and provide an institute of learning. As I have said several times, Business S.O.S. is an inclusive community. That means everyone who is willing to adhere to our philosophy and requirements to creating a safe, trustworthy business community of the highest level of business ethics and corporate governance can participate. Together we can create a very liquid environment, to resuscitate our businesses and project these American values wherever we are trading and as we expand our businesses globally.

      I did want to focus on the three most important marketing avenues, namely, TV, Internet, and Mobile devices because that is where our customers are viewing our messaging currently and at least into the near future.

      TV provides a unique opportunity to develop branded content and integrated marketing that creates a rich, deep, three-dimensional vehicle for all products and services. The Internet knows that consumers still rely on visiting a website for the complete story of each brand. And the Mobile device, which soon will become an appendage, will keep all of our banking and financials and purchase capability, house our business files through cloud computing, and entertain us with HD brilliance for watching streaming videos for pure enjoyment. Apps are strong tools to establish a connection that is so important to create the 24/7 instant service and supply capability.

After being one of the largest print media buying firms in the South East, while I was retooling my firm I decided that along with a focus on all three digital screens I would enhance my marketing position by adding activist marketing to this communication mix. Take for instance our position on the type of marketing we now accept. My firm declines doing any more print advertising. This time I want to be ahead of the curve--and make a clear statement about our environment. The destruction of our forest and the enormous amount of carbon in the atmosphere: cutting and bring these trees to paper mills and then to the end user markets is something I want no longer to encourage.

Perhaps I will acquiesce to a business card, but only when necessary and one that is unique. Unlike years ago when I did a vast amount of corporate stationary packages, I think anyone can get a personalized card from Vista Print for ten dollars. I cannot do better than that. Let's begin as marketers to understand that paper is a natural resource we should use sparingly.

Business S.O.S.™

Also, my position on activist marketing is part of the brand development that Business S.O.S. wants all of it participants to embrace. It will be emphasized in all of our volunteerism. Member companies, which have the opportunity to be re-designed, will be invited to develop something in their product or services line that pays forward in a way that makes sense to them. This is the nature of being American. We need to bring back the passion we all felt or feel about helping our neighbor. God Bless America.

Chapter 7
Bankruptcy is a Scourge for Small Business and Not An Option

New research indicates that one of the best ways to encourage people to start and stay in business is to have lenient bankruptcy laws. We need to send the message that it's okay to fail, especially in the wake of a near economic collapse of our financial system.[1]

Entrepreneurs power the American economy. They enter and exit in a continuous, harmonious process that Joseph Schumpeter in 1942 called "creative destruction, the essential fact about capitalism."

When he wrote this, one-third of new businesses died in the first two years; when I started my business in 1989, about 50 percent were able to survive to year five or beyond. Now most fail, and it is estimated as high as 90 percent in some states. The federal bankruptcy laws in Schumpeter's day were written so that the entrepreneur could bounce back. This policy is no longer available. With the disparity of income, a shrinking consumer base, and lack of capital and investment, our policy makers refused to see that the deck is stacked against entrepreneurs. As a result, the numbers of bankruptcies has more than doubled since 1994.[2]

Now the majority fails to survive. Until 2008, new business births always exceeded deaths. Now the number of deaths to small enterprise is at a frightening level. Please see the chart in Chapter 1 for more information.

Despite such odds, the number of new entrants has been increasing slightly in the first and second quarters of 2013. How do we help this increase over time? How do we encourage the serial entrepreneur to thrive, resurfacing, again and again, if he, or she, so desires? And, the millions still in survival mode after the recession need to regain strength in a continuously fragile and changed economy. How do we coax them out of hibernation? Remember, small businesses account for more than 99 percent of all enterprises in the United States, close to 51 percent of all employment, and 65 percent of new hires. Small business success is tied to our economic recovery and the health of our nation.

> **How Important are Small Businesses to the U.S. Economy?**
>
> **Small firms**:
> - Represent 99.7 percent of all employer firms
> - Employ about half of all private sector employees
> - Pay 43 percent of total U.S. private payroll
> - Have generated 65 percent of the net new jobs over the past 17 years
> - Create more than half of the nonfarm private GDP
> - Hire 43 percent of high tech workers
> - Are 52 percent home-based and 2 percent franchises
> - Made up 97.5 percent of all identified exporters and produced 31 percent of export value in FY 2008
> - Produce 16.5 times more patents per employee than large patenting firms
> - Employ 65% of all new hires.

Much of the national policy debate about small business focuses, rightly, on firms that can survive. Taxes, healthcare costs, capital growth, and the like are generated by businesses that have more than minimal incomes, employees on their payrolls, and investment options. But what about firms that don't make it? How do we treat entrepreneurs who fail? What is the lasting effect on our American psychic and Brand America? The latest research suggests that this may be a turning point in the U.S. as so many companies are filing for bankruptcy or merely closing their doors at an alarming rate.

Over the years, America's personal bankruptcy system has served as a hedge against entrepreneurial failure. When businesses fail, entrepreneurs can shield some of their assets from creditors by filing under Chapter 7 of the federal bankruptcy laws, the usual route for consumer filings. In fact, nearly 20 percent of all personal filings list business debts, and the value of business debts represents half the total liabilities of bankruptcy filers. But, entrepreneurs are seldom the focus of debates about bankruptcy reform, because the process rarely distinguishes consumers from small business owners. This lack of understanding is the flaw in these new policies.

America's bankruptcy law is rooted in the "fresh start" - the idea that honest debtors experiencing a spot of bad luck, such as temporary job loss, illness, or divorce, are capable of putting the past behind them and moving on. This concept works especially well for owners of small businesses. By wiping out debts and pardoning failure, American bankruptcy gives the entrepreneur a chance to bounce back and even be worry free, if he really screws up, and an opportunity to learn from his/her mistakes.

Bankruptcy is a Scourge!

It's no surprise that these laws--seen as lenient not just by creditors but by our policy makers influenced by these creditors' lobbyists–have increasingly become a subject of debate in recent times.

There is a growing fear that the system is too harsh to debtors, and there is evidence that this could be, potentially, crushing our entrepreneurship. The number of Americans seeking relief from creditors each year has more than doubled in the past decade to almost two million. This steady and rapid rise in bankruptcy filings has coincided with a generally robust economy as is reflected in our graph from 1994.

Quarterly Non-Business Bankruptcy Filings by Chapter (1994 - 2012)

Year	Total	Chapter 7	Chapter 11	Chapter 13	Percentage of Chapter 7 Filings
1994	780,455	537,551	2,265	240,639	68.88%
1995	874,642	597,048	1,369	276,225	68.26%
1996	1,124,286	779,128	1,170	343,987	69.30%
1997	1,349,510	956,607	1,071	391,832	70.89%
1998	1,397,695	1,007,471	861	389,363	72.08%
1999	1,281,360	909,719	2,783	377,640	71.00%
2000	1,217,628	838,576	686	378,366	68.87%
2001	1,101,808	1,031,238	789	419,660	93.60%
2002	1,537,730	1,086,459	984	450,277	70.65%
2003	1,624,677	1,155,081	954	467,908	71.10%
2004	1,562,621	1,117,304	960	444,352	71.50%
2005	2,039,214	1,631,011	877	407,322	79.98%
2006	597,965	349,012	520	248,430	58.37%
2007	822,590	500,613	617	321,359	60.86%
2008	1,074,225	714,389	888	358,947	66.50%
2009	1,412,838	1,008,870	1,506	402,462	71.41%
2010	1,536,799	1,100,116	1,939	434,739	71.58%
2011	1,362,847	958,634	1,757	402,454	70.34%
2012	916,270	639,880	1,121	275,266	69.78%

Quarterly Business Bankruptcy Filings by Year
(1994 - 2012)

Year	1st Quarter	2nd Quarter	3rd Quarter	4th Quarter	Total
1994	13,858	13,617	12,878	12,021	52,374
1995	13,123	12,216	12,648	12,891	51,878
1996	13,388	13,992	13,198	12,887	53,465
1997	13,831	13,991	13,456	12,653	53,931
1998	12,410	11,552	10,346	9,888	44,196
1999	9,180	10,378	8,986	9,020	37,564
2000	9,456	9,243	8,211	8,413	35,472
2001	10,005	10,330	9,537	10,013	40,099
2002	9,775	9,695	9,433	9,500	38,540
2003	8,814	9,331	8,446	8,294	35,037
2004	10,566	8,249	7,574	7,778	34,317
2005	8,063	8,736	9,476	12,798	39,201
2006	4,086	4,858	5,284	5,586	19,695
2007	6,280	6,705	7,167	7,985	28,322
2008	8,713	9,743	11,504	12,901	43,546
2009	14,319	16,014	15,177	15,020	60,837
2010	14,607	14,452	13,957	13,030	56,282
2011	12,376	12,304	11,705	11,149	47,806
2012	10,998	10,374	9,248		

This is a clear alert that the disparity in income on Main Street was affecting small business owners and their consumer base way before the Great Recession. Yet, either our lawmakers never saw these parallels, or large corporations and banks blinded them.

Under pressure from creditor groups, including banks and credit card companies, Congress, in 2005, passed the Bankruptcy Abuse, Fraud, Prevention, and Consumer Protection Act, which make debtors jump through many more bureaucratic hoops to get relief. Signing the act, President Bush said, "In recent years, too many people have abused the bankruptcy laws. They've walked away from debts, even when they had the ability to repay them. This has made credit less affordable and less accessible." Yet, in an attempt to re-gauge the imbalance, the debate on bankruptcy has neglected the implications of such legislation for entrepreneurial behavior.[3]

Does bankruptcy regulation affect entrepreneurship? My own research, along with that of Michelle J. White, professor of economics at the University of California at San Diego, answers with an unequivocal "yes." Studying variations in laws across the country, we find that States that, more extensively, protect the assets of those filing for bankruptcy, have a higher percentage of business start-ups and survival rates. Thus, the more a state forgives its debtors, the greater the entrepreneurial dynamism in that state.[4]

Entrepreneurship is often a process of trial and error. No one would accuse Henry Ford of being an unsuccessful entrepreneur. But, Ford started two car companies that failed before he struck gold with the Ford Motor Company. Sometimes we fail at no fault of our own, as is the case for over 5.8 million citizens/businesses that filed between 2008 and 2012 (reference chart, below), just after the so-called Great Recession or Depression. If you know that your home and personal property will be protected no matter what the outcome of your venture, you are more likely to take the risk of starting a business in the first place and to try again if you don't succeed. States like Texas, Nevada, and Delaware, with high personal bankruptcy exemptions, offer a better environment for businesses than Maryland or Virginia, with relatively low exemptions. The right to go bust is an insurance policy against financial disaster. These policies have under gone drastic changes since 2005.

States are less likely to see high entrepreneurship rates if their exemptions are lower than those of neighboring states. After all, entrepreneurs are free to move across state lines and take advantage of more lenient exemptions. Just as people vote with their feet by moving to states with lower taxes and better schools, entrepreneurs move to states with better bankruptcy regulations and better business conditions.

These findings warn that bankruptcy reform must proceed with care and especially with a better understanding of the role bankruptcy plays for small businesses. But, the 2005 law seems to be moving in the wrong direction. It introduced a slew of new provisions to make it harder for individuals to file for bankruptcy or businesses to survive once they have filed. According to the latest data, only 10 percent of all companies that file Chapter 11 actually survive. Most are forced later to dissolve under a Chapter 7 filing--death at the end of a prolonged illness.

United States bankruptcy courts - Bankruptcy bases filed/commenced, terminated, and pending

March 31, 2007 – June 30, 2013

Year	Fillings	Percent Change	Terminations	Percent Change	Pending	Percent Change
2007	695,575	---	950,845	---	1,364,516	---
2008	901,927	+29.7	904,207	-4.9	1,284,614	-0.2
2009	1,202,395	+33.3	1,073,619	+18.7	1,418,472	+10.0
2010	1,531,997	+27.4	1,353,528	+26.1	1,596,990	+12.6
2011	1,571,183	+2.6	1,512,011	+11.7	1,659,874	+3.7
2012	1,367,006	-13.0	1,385,725	-8.4	1,641,127	-1.1
2013	1,137,978	-13.2	1,215,118	-10.3	1,585,516	-4.6

For instance, only those with incomes below the state median can claim asset protection under Chapter 7, others must either devise a repayment plan out of future earnings under Chapter 11 or not file at all. Exemptions have been lowered for certain assets, and debtors need to undergo credit counseling prior to filing, a process that can be costly, humiliating, and, for many business owners, useless. A better approach would be to let creditors work through the market to ensure that debtors with bad credit history or risky entrepreneurial ventures are given loans at higher interest rates. Also, creditors could issue more secured debt to ensure repayment.[5]

If entrepreneurs of failed businesses are denied debt discharge, they may take up safer wage and salary jobs rather than risk starting up a new venture. We can all end up working for big global conglomerates or the government. Another unintended consequence of the legislation, therefore, maybe the loss of another Henry Ford, Steve Jobs, or Bill Gates, me, or you, or anyone with a dream and a vision, however big or small. And lowering the level of asset protection provided to homes and personal property means even higher stakes for start-ups, deterring would-be entrepreneurs from risking creative destruction. In the case of the impact of the 2005 laws, it could mean a change from creative destruction to extinction of the American Entrepreneur. With fewer entrepreneurs we move toward socialism and jeopardize the great experiment upon which democracy was built.[6]

For the millions of firms on survival mode the need to retool and resuscitate your business is of paramount

Bankruptcy is a Scourge!

importance before you slip into bankruptcy because of this new policy. This is why I call bankruptcy reform one of the social imperatives of our times. There is a profoundly negative impact from these drastic changes in the law on small-firms entry decisions and current firms' options to regroup. It is simply scary as hell out there and bankruptcy has caused untold suffering to millions of entrepreneurs.

A sad irony of the 2005 legislation is that, while many countries are learning from an American system that is seen widely as the world's most friendly to entrepreneurs, America seems not to be heeding its own lessons. One of the reasons I wrote this book is because I saw from the data on bankruptcy that the American Dream is dying because of these very policies. The total lack of understanding or concern of our lawmakers is why we need to develop a system or network to help each other navigate through these tumultuous times. We also need to communicate openly the consequences of policies that kill the dreams of so many.[7]

Do we really want to move toward a system where failure is feared and the entrepreneurial spirit takes a beating at every turn? Or, on the other hand, do we want to tell our entrepreneurs that there is hope on its way when they are in S.O.S. and provide the tools and support needed to get out of this mess through the help of an open source of resources.

History teaches us that entrepreneurship involves a process of learning and experimentation; failure may well be a crucial part of this process. These quantum structural changes are complex and involve great risk even more so then in the past for small enterprise. Expanding markets, testing new ways of developing products, communicating in new media, reinventing yourself and trying something completely new--these are all about innovation and experimentation. As a society and an economy, our best asset may be our ability to accept and forgive. So each time we tighten our bankruptcy laws in response to the legions of lawyers, large banks, and credit card companies, we have to wonder if we are not, inadvertently, reducing America to Rome.

Marke Leibovich's new book is *This Town*, which takes down what he calls the creatures who infest our nation's capital. Christopher Buckley's review states, "*This Town* reads like the endgame chapters of Gibbon's *Decline and Fall of the Roman Empire*." In it, he discusses the tectonic changes that have occurred in the past 40 years, number one being the near complete takeover of our elected officials by lobbyists of special interests. In President

Obama's first year, it seems to have reached a record of $3.47 billion. This has led to the latest figure for Congressional approval at 12 percent, its lowest ever. In 1973, only 3 percent of retiring members of Congress became lobbyists. "Now 50 percent of Senators and 42 percent of Congressmen join the ranks of influence peddlers because the cash rewards are so large and it is their bounty for their largess while they were in public service."[8] How can we expect our elected officials to govern and enact policy that will perpetuate our entrepreneurship when it is clear for whom they are really working?

    Leibovich goes on to write that corporate America, mostly Wall Street and the large banks, have tripled the amount of money they spend on lobbying and public affairs. Along with that is the tsunami of dollars thrown at presidential campaigns by so-called PAC's and mega-donors of over $2 billion dollars. Who are we kidding? This is corruption at the highest level. We are literally rotting from the inside out. Yet, these are the very lawmakers that have no mercy when a small business--with limited resources and facing an insurmountable shift in our economic system find themselves in debt and struggling. I guess we should have known. But, so many of us did not see it coming.

This chapter is a wakeup call that bankruptcy is not an option for small business, but a scourge. All of the talk of a "fresh star" and a "salvation" is the language of law firms who want your business in order to collect large fees. Once you sign their engagement letter the veil begins to be lifted to expose a very brutal process. Many people commit suicide, need counseling, or never start a business again as a result.

Bankruptcy law, seemingly by design, is one of the most confusing areas of the law. It is billed as a protection but in fact, it is a very destructive process both financially and psychologically. It can thrust a small business because of inadequate counsel into greater expense and could last for years. Which is why I became so alarmed at the sheer numbers of our entrepreneurial brothers and sister going through this hell every year. I believe it is because there is a complete lack of awareness of how vial this process can be for most businesses that file under Chapter 7 or 11 Protection. Even the name is misleading.[9]

Under Chapter 7 of the bankruptcy code, you liquidate your business and the sale of those assets helps pay your creditors. The area that gets grey is that most large institutions--especially credit card companies in their fine print--hold you personally liable for any business expenses even though the card is under your business name. Hence, you are then forced to shift course and file on a personal level, and that places every personal asset in jeopardy of liquidation including the shirt off your back. Unfortunately, asset protection should begin the day you start your business or decide on the status of your company. If your counsel does not explain this thoroughly and you are not forth coming, or if you don't include even the paper clips on the filing schedule, then the new law states you are committing federal fraud and could serve up to 20 years in prison. I'll bet most lawyers selling you on going bankrupt don't tell you that or veil the process until you sign the engagement letter or perhaps even more egregiously fail to mention it after you file."[10]

They go as far as assigning a Trustee of the courts who gets a "commission" for finding you in a compromising situation. They could spend years suing you for questionable assets and many businesses relinquish assets simply because there are no resources to defend the assets in question. This is what most business owners are not aware of. During the time a business owner feels compelled to file generally, he or she is too humiliated and demoralized to ask around as to who is the best attorney his fellow associates may know in order to submit such a complex and serious filing. We all know that without money we cannot find the quality of service we need when we need it. Many struggling entrepreneurs read the veiled sales pitch on the lawyer's website that it is the only way to a "fresh start" and believe it could be the answer to their problems. In fact, it could be the beginning of a process that is short of a death by torture. It is evident that I am neither an expert nor a lawyer and in a need to continue my research on this hidden tragedy that is happening at an alarming rate to our citizenry. However, I intend to expose the true nature of this misguided change in the laws and policy of corporate and personal bankruptcy. Thousands of small businesses are simply uninformed and suffer severe consequences as a result.

 Chapter 11 bankruptcy states that you can rehabilitate your business by reorganizing your debt in agreement with your creditors. Yet, 95 percent of all companies who file Chapter 11 file for Chapter 7 shortly thereafter because Chapter 11 simply does not provide the help that a struggling small business needs in today's dysfunctional economy. It is such a systemic multi-faceted problem that it only adds to the suffering of small business owners and complicates their already severe problems. For the lawyers who promote it, it simply spells big fees. If they read at all, then they are more than aware at the grim results of such a filing provides for their clients.[11]

Statistics reveal that the few companies that survive Chapter 11 are usually large companies. Donald Trump has declared bankruptcy four times and utilizes it as a business tool. He has a legion of attorneys, which, of course, plan for the bankruptcy in advance for many of his development projects in order to increase his own personal wealth. This practice in general has driven many small sub-contractors out of business, bidding already on very low margins because of competition and forced later to settle for pennies on the dollar creating the cash poor scenario that could drive a small contractor over the edge. This is all a legal corporate practice: gaming the system, providing even the bankruptcy code to be written for the benefit of large corporations thanks to lobbyists taking part in the writing of this policy. All is part of business as usual in Washington.

The small businessman cannot resolve all of his problems in Chapter 11 bankruptcy. It is a strong medicine for a sick business. For many a small company, it is too strong a medicine that could kill you.

Chapter 9 Quarterly Filings (1980-2012)
Municipality Bankruptcy

Year	1st Quarter	2nd Quarter	3rd Quarter	4th Quarter	Total
1980	-	-	1	-	1
1981			2		2
1982		2	1		3
1983	1	1	2		4
1984	1	1	2		4
1985	1		1	1	3
1986	1	4	1	2	8
1987	5	2			7
1988	1	2	1	1	5
1989	2	3	2	2	9
1990	2	1	6	4	13
1991	6	5	2	5	18
1992	6	2	5	1	14
1993	2	1	4	5	12
1994	5	3	3	5	16
1995	3	1	1	5	10
1996	2	2	4		8
1997	1	5	4		10
1998	-	1	1	1	3
1999	1		2	2	5
2000	2	2	3	4	11
2001		2	3	3	8
2002		3	2	2	7
2003		3	-	3	6
2004	2	2	1	2	7
2005	1	2	4	4	11
2006	2		1	2	5
2007	2	2	1	1	6
2008		2	1	1	4
2009	3	1	2	6	12
2010	1	2	2	1	6
2011	2	2	3	6	13
2012	2	6	9		

NOTE: The purpose of chapter 9 is to provide a financially distressed municipality protection from its creditors while it develops and negotiates a plan for adjusting its debts. The term "municipality" is defined in the Bankruptcy Code as a "political subdivision or public agency or instrumentality of a State." 11 U.S.C. § 101(40). The definition is broad enough to include cities, counties, townships, school districts, and public improvement districts. It also includes revenue-producing bodies that provide services, which are paid for by users, rather than by general taxes, such as bridge authorities, highway authorities, and gas authorities.

Not only is this systemic problem part of the aftermath of the failure of our financial system resulting in countless home foreclosures, and personal and business bankruptcies, it is also alarmingly on the rise for our municipalities.

Bankruptcy is a Scourge!

We have talked about the cause and effect that our failing small businesses have had on so many aspects of our society, but one of the most serious is the bubble I believe that is about to burst and that is, that with the failure of our businesses comes the failure of our municipalities.

In 1980, we had one bankruptcy filing for a municipality. In 2012, for some reason, there is no recording for the fourth quarter, but the three proceeding quarters add up to 17. If we average the last five years, the percentage of increase would estimate at least 3 more for fourth quarter 2012, totaling twenty municipalities filing Chapter 9 bankruptcy.

Twenty U.S. cities are in such financial duress that they are forced to file. In looking at the total U.S. budget and seeing that pensions comprise 22 percent, debt and even municipal loans are bundled and packaged as derivatives; many of our cities do not have the revenue to support this large liability. It can only make one worry about the continued volatility and fragility of who is betting that these loans will burst. We have seen this before in the way the real estate bubble burst and the last financial bubble burst setting us on a course that has created the largest disparity in wealth even greater than the Gilded Age. Europe is in far greater straights than the U.S. There is no comfort in feeling we can fend off becoming Greece, however, if we do not make great and ardent efforts to reclaim and ignite the little engine that could--our small businesses. With the health of our entrepreneurs, we will generate the revenue for our cities.

It is unconscionable that in 2013, Detroit, once our fourth largest municipality, has filed Chapter 9 when Congress has been more than happy to spend $3 Billion a month for nation building in Iraq in the not so distant past. If we cannot save one of our largest cities--one, which housed one of our biggest industries--how are we going to lead the world in capitalism and democracy?

On a more optimistic note, many of our cities are fighting back. In a recent article, Thomas Freidman writes how the most exciting innovation in governance is happening in many American cities. "The country looks so much better from the bottom up." He talks about a metropolitan explosion quoting scholars from the Brookings Institute: Bruce Katz and Jennifer Bradley expounding on "The Metropolitan Revolution: How Cities and Metros Are Fixing Our Broken Politics and Fragile Economy." There is a trend that many cities are becoming the leaders in the nation by experimenting and taking risks calling it "the inversion of the hierarchy of power."[12]

The Great Recession accelerated the changes to our traditional growth model. "One that exalted consumption over production, speculation over investment and waste over sustainability." The new growth model, which most successful cities are practicing, focuses on creating networks.

"They combine skilled labor and knowledgeable workers with universities and technical schools, enhance the quality of infrastructure and high speed Internet, promote manufacturing, innovation, technology, and advanced service with an eye for exporting all of these."10 These cities understand that they have to have a sector of their city that is world class. That is how a 21st Century city builds a strong middle class, and prevents the coarsening of society and all of the ills that surround it from taking hold. He is quoted as saying: "Cities and metropolitan areas are on their own! Mired in partisan division and rancor the federal government seems incapable of taking bold action to restructure our economy and grapple with changing demography and rising inequality." 11 These cities are not waiting for, but are trying to grow, their economies on their own.

This in fact is what I have been addressing to small business entrepreneurs before I read Friedman's article.

Business S.O.S.™

This bottom up approach and transfer of the hierarchy of power could be the same momentum we can now establish through Business S.O.S. and its network of members, sponsors, resources, volunteers and struggling businesses.

Business S.O.S. is a network established because "Washington and Wall Street seem to be functioning on their own with little or no regard to what is happening to everyday Americans." It is a way for a specific sector of struggling entrepreneurs to get the level of help they need when they need it. Many of us have endured little or no growth for five long years. This can be an economically stressful situation, but bankruptcy as I have outlined, in many cases is not the answer. Business S.O.S. is a place entrepreneurs can go without hiding from the harsh facts of their reality. There is no judgment or shame, but understanding and assessment of your total corporate DNA in order to protect your business from sliding into bankruptcy. I am a believer that every company is worth saving. As long as the company can eventually profit, there is always a chance to sell and become part of a larger entity that can produce greater challenges and opportunities.

One of the preeminent lessons I have learned about business is that right from the beginning, your business and your personal assets need to be protected in case something dreadful happens, and you are forced into bankruptcy.

Your business is always vulnerable to litigation and creditors. The boom-bust economies will continue to occur, perhaps even more frequently if Washington doesn't fix the systemic problems that we have discussed. Financial threats are looming all the time and can sink your business as we have seen from our data effecting millions of businesses. After experiencing five separate economic traumas in the last ten years, we can assume from this pattern they will keep on coming. It is so important that businesses retool and reduce the risk of failure. It has become a necessity to safeguard your enterprise in order to survive in these turbulent times. Hillel Presser, in Financial Self-Defense, addresses a trend that is clearly on the rise: to not incorporate or file any business status, but to remain a sole proprietor. According to some recent figures from the SBA, this is confirmed from their recent data.

Business S.O.S.™

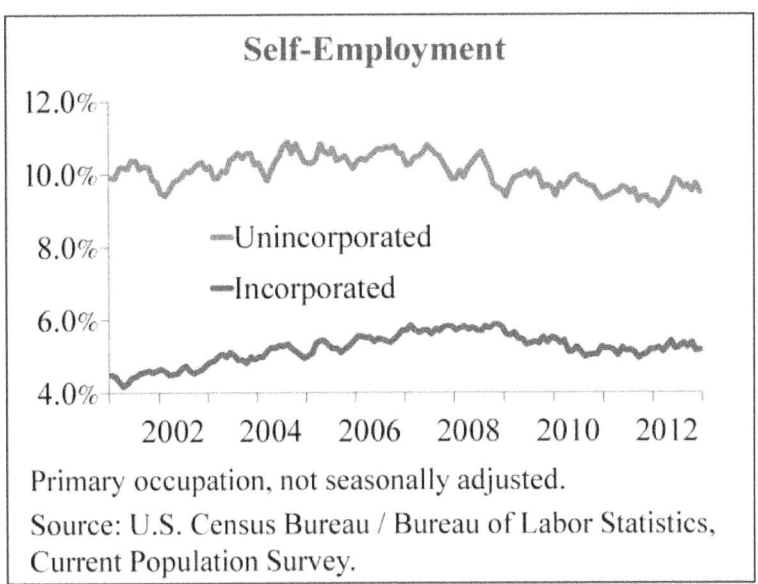

Primary occupation, not seasonally adjusted.
Source: U.S. Census Bureau / Bureau of Labor Statistics, Current Population Survey.

He explains, "There is a case to be made against sole proprietorships as a sole proprietor is personally liable for every business debt." Yet we see an increase in unincorporated self-employment. People are sensing the punishment they will withstand if their corporation fails. When most small businesses now fail, it is putting in jeopardy the entire family's financial security. Presser goes on to say: "It is very foolish, and no business is too small to need to incorporate or form a Limited Liability Company."[13]

We will develop an app to guide new ventures on this decision-making process. The vision is to garner the help of experienced sponsors, such as Hillel. We will also provide the capability to evaluate the current status of the business filing to keep up with these new economic forces which may be making the simple corporate status for some obsolete and the need to change to an LLC may be a necessity. The complete redesign of your business for 21st Century business makes this an important part of the process. And, because so many businesses are failing, we need to impart knowledge and a real understanding of the liabilities you are now facing in continued pervasive survival mode.

This book was written primarily to take the blinders off the eyes of small business owners to encourage them to look at the economic facts and assess their struggles not only within the small microcosm of their current life experience but also through the wide angle lenses of all the mitigating reasons they cannot change their state of affairs and resuscitate their businesses so easily. These issues function within two, totally separate economies. The inability of small entrepreneurs to avoid much longer with the devastating effects of bankruptcy may in fact change our revered capitalism involuntarily to socialism because of the inequality and the unleveled playing field between large corporations, the enormous wealth of the top one percent of companies and individuals, and the economic distress of the bottom 99 percent. Clearly what I am saying is that large corporations and monopolies, which are considered the beacon of capitalism, are the strongest and most competitive force. These are the catalyst for more rapid "natural destruction" of smaller competitors. Maybe this is the very reason we are moving toward socialism and not that the bottom half is lazy and looking to be opportunistic seekers of social services.

Joseph Schumpeter is perhaps best known for his book, Capitalism, Socialism, and Democracy. His theory is that capitalism could collapse and be replaced by socialism. "Creative destruction" is the process in which the old ways of doing things are endogenously destroyed and replaced by new ways.[14]

The success of capitalism will lead to a form of "corporatism" and foster values hostile to capitalism and democracy in which there is a lack of equality and a fair playing field for most innovators or entrepreneurs. He goes on to say: "The intellectual and social climate needed to allow entrepreneurship to thrive will not exist in advanced capitalism or corporatism; it will be replaced by socialism in some form. There will not be a revolution, but merely a trend in the U.S. to elect policy makers of one stripe or another because of the vast needs of the majority against the power of the minority who cannot compete in a corporatist economy and have less income and need more social services and government jobs and subsidies. He argues that the possible collapse of capitalism from within will come about as democratic governments vote for restrictions upon entrepreneurship that will burden and destroy the capitalist structure; the corporatist will choke off the competitive environment making it hostile to smaller companies. He also emphasizes non-political, evolutionary processes in society where "liberal capitalism" was evolving into democratic socialism as the result of all of these imbalances. This is a highbrow discussion that simply states the true consequence of inequality for entrepreneurs. When all the policies are in favor of large corporations and all the regulations are inflicted on all the small organizations the natural trend will be the destruction of democracy and capitalism, as we know it.[15]

This is economic theory that we can see playing out in our country today. I am obviously on the side of most Americans. Policy does affect our very democracy as we see its vast changes. We have time to correct these trends by taking action. I am offering all of the methods utilized in the development of Business S.O.S. in order to correct this unleveled playing field and advantage big corporations now

Business S.O.S.™

have in the expansion of our capitalism through the harnessing of information technology and globalization. We need to network and harness these capacities, and we can correct this imbalance. These challenges and cycle of businesses are ongoing. Business S.O.S. offers the tools to assist small businesses and become part of the new hierarchy of power that is within our reach if we all stop listening to the rhetoric of our politicians and proceed as they did in the early days of this country and help each other like caring and trusted neighbors through the hard times.

Chapter 8
The Way Forward: Ignite Small Businesses and Renew a Sense of Hope

Eckhart Tolle notes our need for radical change: "The more that the dysfunction of the human mind plays itself out on the world stage, clearly visible to everyone in the daily television news reports, the greater the number of people who realize the urgent need for a radical change in human consciousness if humanity is not to destroy both itself and the planet."[1]

Just as this spiritual guru feels compelled to share his enlightened teachings, I find it imperative to expose the true state of America's small businesses. Specifically, Tolle finds resistance to what he calls the "suchness" of the present moment. Now is the fullness of life. At times, I am certain the information I have shared seems harsh, cynical, or much too complicated or even difficult to face. Unfortunately, it is the only way toward creating understanding, knowledge, and a consciousness that fits the reality of our times. We need to acknowledge the dissatisfaction right now in critical mass openly. This is what can bring about the kind of change significant enough to matter to such a large body of businesses right now.

Business S.O.S.™

This Collective Gestalt could foster the dynamic thinking transformative enough to move many millions of businesses forward at the same time. If we all jumped in together as a proactive network, and if we together open-sourced all of our resources and tools, creative thinking and a willingness to work together, utilizing all of the benefits of the digital age and the opportunity to work all across the globe, then we can be successful. If we all surrender (as Tolle discusses) to the possibilities that are *now* that our mutual efforts would achieve together, then it could be a renaissance of sorts for a new kind of entrepreneurship. It is very exciting, uplifting, and offers hope to so many.

Human consciousness, whether spiritual or societal, is the same transformative process that Tolle offers in our desire to evolve into something or someone better. It is the same passion and excitement, which manifested in the enlightened thinkers who fought for our liberty or wrote our constitution to create the greatest republic on earth. It is what galvanized the abolitionist, suffragettes, freedom riders, and gay activists who were successful in their movements for change. The vast inequality of our system as it stands now must go. It is the social imperative of our time. I focus here in this manuscript on small businesses.

True knowledge or consciousness about the dysfunctional economy that many of us are now suffering allows one to recognize what is false or faulty with clarity. This awaking to bring us to a collective "big thinking and collaboration" is part of our culture and history as a country that responds to the needs of its people.

This transformation in the way we compete, collaborate, and communicate is not in the distant future as Tolle reiterates about spiritualism. It is available *now*--no matter who or where you are. Being proud of what you are doing as an individual business and how you are affecting others can create a new American patriotism, if enough businesses speak out, help, and participate.

Change is difficult and frightening. It connotes in some instances defeat, giving up, even failing to rise to the challenges of life or the times. It is so difficult that it sometimes does not occur unless there is a major catastrophe or grave injustice. In my instance it was the death of my business that had been successful for so long that it became a part of my identity, power, and social standing.

It has been a difficult process to reveal openly my failures and the true state of my once successful business. Then I realized it was not just I but millions of small businesses across the country. These power and identity issues happen to many entrepreneurs who passionately built their businesses from nothing. It is also a part of our antiquated corporate culture of secrecy not to share the reality but to keep our suffering close to the vest and it will eventually all go away but this time it just won't happen. The changes are to extreme and the environment too complex and difficult to navigate.

  To watch your business slowly die or disintegrate is distressing for so many. For a long time, I had an unwillingness to accept it and was so unhappy and depressed that I could not rebuild I was immobilized with shock and fear. I became listless, lethargic, and angry, which was totally unlike me. (Like most self-starters, I have always had an intense energy level and a positive attitude toward life) We are a group of highly motivated individuals with unique skills. But, this has been a challenge bigger and deeper than I was able to wrap my arms around until I became informed and acted on that information. Then I was able to save my own business so very close to the precipice of destruction.

  I utilized all of the concepts discussed in these pages, such as partnerships and teaming, marketing on all three screens, and expanding my operation globally. It was also very important I give my new retooled venture an activist component. Business S.O.S. is my way to pay forward. It allows me to utilize the skills I have developed to empower people that have worked for me or with me. This was something that I became aware of after I pitched dozens of businesses and realized they were not hiring me but had learned from me and were able to take what I had taught them and apply it to their business or marketing and more. I have always felt I have an obligation to help my fellow colleagues. In the good times, a necessary part of giving back to the great society that allowed me to achieve the successes I was enjoying. Now it is important to add that important ingredient of meaning to the work that I do after learning from my profound experience of success, failure, and success again. It was a tough road but I have come out the other side feeling grateful and wanting to share this newfound knowledge. I am not in it alone.

  When I started to develop this concept, I took my passion and outrage on the road. I found so many who already know what is going on, but have no tools to help mend our neighbors or ourselves. Helping others re-cycles and helps the stability of our own business. This is why I am developing the proprietary software capable of bringing struggling businesses, sponsors, volunteers, experts, and other guru's together, along with the assets, strengths, expertise, and potential to help each other out of this pervasive mess.

The goal is that Business S.O.S. will provide the assistance, knowledge, and tooling to compete in a larger business arena against all the new and unforeseen mitigating forces currently affecting our economy. Business S.O.S. will help small businesses level the playing field. Each such business will achieve integration and will be allowed into the opportunities of the 21st Century through the help of their neighbor and community. These original American values are as old as the very first settlers who conquered the challenges of prior centuries. By helping each other, we help ourselves as well as take on big challenges together. Business S.O.S. is only the vehicle, the "power of now" is what will ignite the momentum.

Chapter 1 offered a complete outline of the true state of our small businesses today. This is not a panacea; there are pockets of industries that are still feeling no pain. However, the vast majority feels it and fears it every day waiting for the other economic shoe to drop. This is an unsettling feeling when our families' lives are at stake.

Our business leaders and policy makers seem to ignore, completely, all of the credible research, data, and statistics that are readily available to everyone. Chapter 1 gives a complete rundown of the reasons we find ourselves in survival mode after five long years after the Great Recession instead of thriving like our large business counterparts and Wall Street. It shows the reasons that the greatest country on earth is destroying the American dream one business and community at a time--and, thus, the country as a whole. Business S.O.S. creates a sound argument for "thinking big" and joining in a collaborative effort, focusing on our small businesses. It will help facilitate a transformation in the way we compete, collaborate, and communicate. It will invert the hierarchy of power and make changes from the bottom up. What Washington and Wall Street can't, or won't, do for us, we will have to do ourselves.

Since 2008, more than two thirds of U.S. small businesses have suffered tremendous losses: 5.8 million have gone bankrupt and scores have been closed. I am not the only one alarmed by these figures. Even with enormous willpower, we simply cannot pull ourselves out of this survival mode and back into growth.

I have outlined how globalization and information technology have changed and overwhelmed small businesses across the country, and how we need to harness these two unique economic factors like our large business counterparts have, collectively to help restore the American dream. We need to allow America once more to lead in our capital markets. The implication of the research presented in this book is that by ignoring the true job creators and the soul of America--the middle class and small business engine--we will lose our power and stature in the world. The American brand as the land of opportunity will vanish.

It is always difficult to explain and launch a concept. But, the audience is there: over 40,000 people per month Google the term *Business S.O.S.*; its cognates garner 3.4 million searches. From these searches, it revivifies the needs of our entrepreneurial colleagues. It is easier to connect on line than it is to face your neighbor with questions that suggest you have a failing business. It is America's hidden secret. If we continue with this ridiculous cover up, then our small business entrepreneurs are in jeopardy of extinction. Someday, it will be too late to administer the cure.

Business S.O.S. is a place--digital or otherwise--where struggling small businesses can go without recourse, fear, or shame, to completely or partially redesign their business for the 21st Century. It is not an advice corner offering suggestions or consultation for a fee; it is not a switch-and-bate operation, but an open source collaboration of resources through proprietary software for businesses in SOS.

It takes the disadvantages of facing less consumer demand, lack of capital, need to retool and enhance IT, modern effective marketing, and a variety of other critical components. It makes their acquisition and implementation obtainable--even while our economy continues to be dysfunctional and devoid of growth.

These complicated structural changes need our community response. Thinking big and formulating a collaborative effort from the bottom-up to redesign our small businesses--one company and community at a time-- will enable the small business owner to compete with our large business counter-parts on the global stage and grow our GDP. Rather than outsource one minute, then call for in-sourcing another, Business S.O.S. stops the merry-go-round and evaluates if these businesses can restructure to partake in the global market or perhaps retool to manufacture quality American made goods and restore manufacturing jobs here, when appropriate. Instead of guessing, we will solicit sponsors, experts, volunteers, and staff who will coordinate these redesigns on a local, regional, and national basis.

You will be able to interface with appropriate colleagues for partnerships to produce or sell in expanded markets. How? Through technology across the channels as many businesses are awakened to an economic nationalism, restoring true corporate governance and trust in our fellow colleagues.

If we are to grow, then we need to work together and trust each other once more. That is the reason when you sign a membership agreement; it is not just riddle with indemnifications and protections on our behalf, but a two-sided real commitment to adhere to all of the rules of corporate governance and ethics--values that were offered on a handshake in decades past. This is a mandatory part of membership, and this will be subject to the necessary review ratings that digital data make so easy. You will know if his membership agreement and his score, reviews and history can trust the business offering service to you in advance. This will enable us to work faster in our quest to make these big changes rapidly before it is too late.

Small business needs more from Washington than a call for tax breaks. It is absurd when so many businesses are in survival mode for a long five years. Small businesses need to be the priority. We all admire Face Book, Microsoft,

Apple, and more. Small businesses that can retool and grow against all odds should be admired just as much.

Small business needs enactment and enforcement of policies and laws that will once again level the playing field for growth among all sectors, not just large corporations. Anti-trust laws are almost completely ignored. Intellectual property is stolen with no recourse. Regulations interfere with productivity. More individuals produce patents, but how can they afford to sue a large company with an army of legal advisers and lobbyists in Washington? The small business without significant help will not survive these unfair practices.

Small businesses are pressured by these large structural changes that have taken place--IT, globalization, and continued dysfunction of the capital and financial markets. The world is flat, and we must help each business view these changes as opportunities, not as recipes for obsolescence.

There are many businesses that know they are already in SOS. Yet facing this may be the biggest hurdle for so many. I know it was for me. Now there is a chance to do something about it. Here are some questions to consider:

- What is the state of your company?

- Do you have the capital to hold on through this continued decrease and lack of confidence in consumer spending?
- What is your sales-to-debt ratio?
- How advanced is the hardware and software you are using?
- How are your sales? (Sales and margins are the fuel to staying alive and your very reason for being.)
- Is your staff trained in management and operation of all digital offerings?
- How are your margins verses overhead and investment capital?
- How tech savvy is you as the owner?
- Can you maintain a 24/7 optimal customer service operation?
- How service-oriented is your accounting division?
- And how good is your product, service, and marketing?
- Can you keep up when the watchword is speed, speed, and speed?

The Way Forward

- Can you maintain that "can do" attitude you had when you started you're firm, or are you depressed and have the business blahs?
- Are you overwhelmed with all of the above?

These are some of the critical questions you need to ask to decide if you are in SOS and need an open source of resources to help.

There is a flurry of new books addressing the financial and psychological stress on small business, the dysfunction of our economy, unmanaged globalization, and poorly resourced IT. Yet, there are few positioned to take action within the confines of the challenges presented. The key to moving from survival mode to growth will be a direct result of the network or partnerships companies are able to forge and their ability to communicate these goods or services through technology to consumers locally to globally. As a network, we can offer the resources and capability to begin the process of action steps to redesign businesses for the 21st Century.

Business S.O.S. has just launched this progressive business model to reorganize. Retool, rehire, train, and get the zeal back. This will need time to grow organically. During this time, we are committed to helping one company at a time to redesign their business for the 21st Century. We offer an open source of resources so that companies can advance their growth on their own.

The 21st Century will be the century of partnerships. Most companies are unable to house all of the disciplines and resources under one roof for a variety of reasons. Through smart equipment and technology, we can forge partnerships with many companies to deliver high quality production and services without suffering the costs and time to retool. Building and developing partnerships are complicated and rout with legal consequences. Business S.O.S. is going to streamline this process. For example, you can partner or collaborate with firms on one or many projects and need not be concerned about the backlash of doing business with someone you do not know. The positive effect of quick, uncomplicated business partnerships set up with limited complication and liability will have a profound effect on growth.

Business S.O.S. is one of many network resources available. We feel our point of difference is that we are not an advice corner, but a way to actually implement the variety of changes a company would need to get out of SOS and back into a growth mode of operation. We expect others to develop and we will create a website to house all of these resources. We are an inclusive business model, not an exclusive club. Everyone is invited to the party of reshaping America's small businesses.

There is only one word that describes many small businesses' understanding, adaptation, and knowledge surrounding the information technology revolution-- *overwhelmed*. I have presented a variety of comprehensive branding campaigns under my digital arm DJS 3SOP (three screens, zero paper). Most firms were aware of marketing online and through digital devices, but few had adequate knowledge as to how to optimize these resources to meet their sales and marketing goals and objectives. They equated it to balls bouncing. They pick up one up, and ten more are thrown their way. Which ones are right for them is anyone's guess. From the analysis of most media plans for the average small business, the depth and results fall short. Seasoned CTOs with real knowledge are few and far between. I have tried to address what components are essential for establishing optimal digital marketing resources. The Business S.O.S. website will categorize thousands of marketing firms and how to set up partnerships with them. We will establish guidelines to develop a first-class multimedia program and produce creative through this network of resources for various categories of industry and service.

    Never before in the history of small business is there a more cost effective way to communicate and seek new customers from all over the world. Marketing is the most important tool to let people know you are out there. It has radically changed since 2008. We discussed in Chapter 5 the relevance of Three Screens - Zero Paper (3S0P) marketing. It explains all aspects of the Internet and mobile devices as well as the use of the Internet and social media on sales, growth, and branding. We intend to develop an online training center so that our network is up to date on all the new trends in media. Staying in front of your customer through these new media offerings is imperative. Mobile first is the imperative, but all three screens are important for small businesses to harness inbound customer communication and sales.

    Video is the fastest growing tool to reach consumers. It is a compelling medium suited for dissemination across all channels. Everyone is enticed to watch video on smart phones and tablets. The small business needs to have resources to produce their own video on-demand and cost effectively. Business S.O.S. will provide the best resources in your area or across the globe that will help produce and distribute this new powerful marketing tool. Video is not just for large companies. It is now important to stream messages in this format if we are to keep up with viewer trends.

There are many reasons small businesses are in survival mode. In the sphere of a small business's corporate control, one of the reasons the U.S. finds itself in 1.2 percent growth is the lack of preparedness, education, and training for the quantum changes that have occurred recently to just about every business model that exists. There are profound changes in software and hardware, communication, finance, production, and more. Is your firm up to date on these changes? Can you afford to re-tool? Are your marketing efforts capable of netting the consumer that will meet your growth goals? Is your physical plant capable of enhancing productivity? Just about every aspect of every business needs an overhaul in order to face the growth and competition challenges of 21st Century business. How do we compare with operations in China, India, or Brazil? Our cultural thinking could be holding us back rather than economic circumstances. We need to borrow from the Olympic spirit of our American athletes, and get back to competing and winning and leading on the global stage.

Globalization assisted in removing barriers between nations through technology. However, it also resulted in competition for American jobs and manufacturing capability empowering countries such as China, India, and Brazil. Globalization is moving very quickly and has changed the U.S. competitive edge. It has flattened the playing field putting pressure on *all* businesses. Without formidable knowledge and pro-active, reliable methodologies, American small businesses cannot take advantage of the tremendous opportunities globalization could afford many companies. It is obvious that American small businesses do not fully grasp this unique opportunity to lead in free trade. This quantum change will require a whole new public awaking; simplistic methodologies will assist small businesses in the repositioning of their businesses as not just local or national, but "glocal." This, for some, may be the only way they can escape survival mode.

This *is* appropriate for our suburban and rural businesses instead of geographic isolationism. We need to get in the game of globalization before it is too late. We should be providing leadership to the world in global integration of our industries and services. Business S.O.S. will assist all companies in their effort to understand how to transition their firms for this kind of growth opportunity. This will eliminate the time it will take to find the right partnerships to expand your firm globally. Whether it is production service or distribution, our network intends to connect our businesses so that we can take advantage of the tremendous opportunity to go global, but avoid the pitfalls logistically and legally.

Business S.O.S. is one of many network resources available. We feel our point of difference is that we are not an advice corner but a way to actually implement the variety of changes a company would need to get out of SOS and back into a growth mode of operation. We expect other networks to develop, and we will create a website to house all of these resources. We are an inclusive business model, not an exclusive club. Everyone is invited to the party of reshaping America's small businesses.

A love of country is the glue that binds us all together. We need to solve big, hard problems together and return to the ideals set forth by our forbearers that we are free individuals with a sense of community. If the top 1 percent is so adamant to keep their tax breaks let the remaining 99 percent do the hard work and sacrifice it will take to correct this horrible economic slide that has damaged the most advanced overachieving nation in the world. We need to redefine the brand that is truly American as the land of opportunity for all and not just for a few. We must work together as a nation to advance progress.

By igniting a newfound inspiration of nationalism and service to our country, we will affect change one business and one community at a time. We will not let ourselves or our neighbors fail around us. We get it done, but everyone needs to pull together giving and doing whatever it takes. We will make it! We did it before, and we will do it again, as the greatest nation on earth. This is a result of love for our country and true nationalism. Washington is broken, but not the spirit of everyday Americans.

Paying It Forward

We can only solve our problems with a collective response. They are too big to be addressed alone. We propose that small businesses network together, reignite our nationalism, and provide the catalyst to change the forces that are impeding our progress. Business S.O.S. can only provide the service of redesigning businesses by and through the help of other businesses. Their rewards for this help are knowing that they have done the right thing. We will ask all of our businesses from sponsors, resources, networks--and especially those that we assist--to pay forward. This can be done either through their product or service development, or their own activism/volunteerism after they return to growth. We must change individual behavior as well as corporate largess to be based on collaboration and connectivity instead of secrecy, suspicion, and divisiveness. I believe all Americans understand the concept of freedom, capitalism, and its effect on corporate growth, progress, and prosperity. The sharing of that prosperity in ways of assisting our colleagues to learn, change, and grow nets tremendous fulfillment for us all as a nation. This fulfillment to help each other will result in growth of our own GDP that should rewards us all across the board fairly.

    Power and influence in the world will be maintained for future generations. The possibility for a better life for all who participate in achieving these goals will be the results of this untold generosity. This is a large, ambitious task. But we, as a community, have faced much worse in our history and have worked together in our quest for resolution. We need the commitment and the good will of all small businesses to help. Paying forward from our volunteers, sponsors, networked businesses, and organizations that jumped in to help each redesigned small business sets the tone of 21st Century methodologies for growth.

In Conclusion

We have outlined in this book the true state of small businesses today. We have exposed why this dysfunction continues and will continue and how we need to develop new methodologies to take many small businesses out of survival mode and back into growth. Identified are the key challenges for small businesses. First, we need to manage globalization so that we lead, and not follow, these trends. Second, we need to adjust to the information technology revolution so that it enhances our businesses and avoids driving the small business to obsolescence.

How to work collaboratively so that we capitalize on this unique historical moment within the constraints of our national financial limitations

The substance of our network will measure us all. Business S.O.S. offers a vehicle to begin this process. It is driven to redesign businesses within a framework that respects the intellectual property of that business and the individual owner. It will work to regain all of the business and corporate governess that propelled our great nation in the 19th and 20th century, such as honesty, integrity, fairness, good work ethic, and quality of products and services. It will place these high ideals in the new context of 21st Century horizontal collaborative modalities and share with the world what truly makes America the greatest nation in the world. We need to stop being overwhelmed by these quantum shifts in our marketplace and get back to meeting these challenges with big ideas and methods that will keep us competitive and in a position of leadership. We have an incredible track record of building the world's most vibrant economy. We can, and we must, succeed again at these endeavors. We offer our solution--Business S.O.S.

Business S.O.S.™

Notes

Introduction

1.　Joseph Stiglitz, *The Price of Inequality: How Today's Divided Society Endangers Our Future* (W.W. Norton, 2013).

Chapter 1

1.　Tyler Cowen, "What Export-Orientated Means," *The American Interest Magazine*, May 2012. "The Lost Decade of the Middle Class," Pew Research Center. August 22, 2012. Retrieved October 15, 2012 from http://www.pewsocialtrends.org/2012/08/22/the-lost-decade-of-the-middle-class/.
2.　"What is SBA's definition of a small business concern?" United States Small Business Administration. Nd. Retrieved October 14, 2012 from http://www.sba.gov/content/what-sbas-definition-small-business-concern.
3.　"Statistics about business size." United States Census Bureau, August 22, 2012. Retrieved October 15, 2012 from http://www.census.gov/econ/smallbus.html.

U.S. Small Business Administration (2009). "Frequently Asked Questions," Retrieved from http://www.sba.gov/sites/default/files/sbfaq.pdf.

4. The Bureau of Labor Statistics (2012), "Labor Force Statistics from the Current Population Survey (CPS) – July 2012," Retrieved from http://www.bls.gov/cps/.

Bureau of Labor Statistics, Department of Labor. October 5, 2012. Retrieved October 14, 2012 from http://www.bls.gov/news.release/pdf/empsit.pdf The US Census Bureau reports that, as of October 2012, the Unites States homes a population of 314,587,391 people. Bureau of Labor Statistics most recent release on employment of September 2012 reports that the United States has a civilian non-institutional population of 243,772,000 people, which includes all persons 16 years of age and older who reside in the fifty states + the District of Columbia who are not inmates of institutions or on active duty in the Armed Forces. Of these, 155,063,000 are considered part of the labor force while 88,710,000 are not. This gives us a 63.6 percent civilian labor force participation rate. Of our labor force, 142,974,000 are reported as employed with 12,088,000 as unemployed, giving us a 58.7 percent employment-to-population ratio and a 7.8 percent unemployment rate. Of the 142,974,000 people reported as employed, 8,613,000 persons are involuntary part-time workers due to economic reasons. If we readjust the calculations, we conclude that there are 21,701,000 unemployed or underemployed workers in the force giving us a un-/underemployment rate of 13.99 percent. Now, if we consider the marginally attached workers, which included discouraged workers, we end up with 24,218,000 as the figure of unemployed and underemployed individuals and an unemployment rate of 15.61 percent.

5. "Everything to Play For," *The Economist*, October 6, 2012. 15.

6. U.S. FDIC (2012). Selections from the Dodd-Frank Wall Street Reform and Consumer Protection Act. Retrieved from http://www.fdic.gov/regulations/reform/dfa_selections.html.

Alexis Goldstein (2012). Comment Letter to the Financial Regulators Urging Them Towards a

Strong Volcker Rule. Retrieved from http://alexisgo.com/book.html.

Frank Newport (2012). "Americans Anti-Big Business, Big Government," Retrieved from http://www.gallup.com/poll/152096/Americans-Anti-Big-Business-Big-Gov.aspx.

7. Carne Ross, *The Leaderless Revolution: How Ordinary People Will Take Power and Change Politics in the Twenty First Century* (New York, NY: Blue Rider Press, 2011).

8. Census Bureau, Bureau of Labor and Statistics, and the U.S. Small Business Administration (2012), Retrieved from http://www.sba.gov/sites/default/files/sbafq.pdf.

9. Tyler Cowen, "What Export Orientated Means," The American Interest Magazine, May 2012.

10. Charles Murray, "The New American Divide," Wall Street Journal, 01-21-12.

11. Joseph Stiglitz, *The Price of Inequality: How Today's Divided Society Endangers Our Future* (New York: W.W. Norton & Company, 2012).

12. *Ibid.*

13. Adam Liptak (2008). "U.S. Prison Population Dwarfs that of Other Nations," Retrieved from

http//www.nytimes.com/2008/04/23/world/Americas/23ht-23prison.12253738.html.

14. "We Just Decided To," *Newsroom*. HBO. (2012).
15. Summary of data reported by the Office of Advocacy including estimates based on data from the U.S. Department of Commerce and The Census Bureau (2009), and trends from the U.S. Department of Labor, Bureau of Labor Statistics, Business Employment Dynamics (BED).
16. Summary of data collected and available from http://www.uscourts.gov/Statistics/BankruptcyStatistics.aspx.
17. Christopher Chantrill, 2012 and 2011. Data compiled by author. Retrieved from http://www.usfederalbudget.us/federal_budget_detail_fy11bs12012n and http://www.usfederalbudget.us/federal_budget_detail_fy11bs12011n.
18. United States Census. September 12, 2012. Retrieved October 16, 2012 from https://www.census.gov/hhes/www/poverty/about/overview/index.html.
Troy Oxford and Lauren Feeney, 2012. "The Triggers of Economic Inequality," based on

information from "Winner-Take-All Politics," by J. Hacker and P. Pierson. Retrieved from http://billmoyers.com/content/the-triggers-of-economic-inequality/.

19. Summary of data reported by Catherine Mulbrandon and retrieved from http://visualizingeconomics.com/illustratedguide/#.UC1mmkTJIbI.

Chapter 2

1. "Interactive Infographic of the World's Best Countries." *Newsweek*. August 15, 2010. Retrieved from http://www.thedailybeast.com/newsweek/2010/08/15/interactive-infographic-of-the-worlds-best-countries.html.
2. See chapter 1, notes 2, 3.
3. "USDebtClock." USDebtClock.org. (2013). Retrieved from: http://www.usdebtclock.org.
"U.S. and World Population Clock." United States Census Bureau. (2013). Retrieved from: http://www.census.gov/popclock.

"It has been approximated that each American owes about $583,708.43 against the federal deficit, even our infants, by the end of fiscal 2013."

4. Brenda Kreonner, "Made in America, Small Businesses Buck the Off Shore Trend." *Wired Magazine*, February 28, 2011.

5. Thomas Friedman defines *globalization* "as the inexorable integration of markets, transportation and communication systems in a way that is enabling corporations, countries, and individuals to reach around the world faster, deeper, and cheaper than ever before." Thomas L. Friedman and Michael Mandelbaum, *That Used to Be Us: How America Fell behind in the World It Invented and How We Can Come Back* (New York: Farrar, Straus, and Giroux, 2011), Kindle edition.

Chapter 3

1. Armington, Catherine, and Marjorie Odle. "Small Business—How Many Jobs?" *The Brookings Review*, Vol. 1, No. 2. (1982).

2. "Moving America's Small Businesses and Entrepreneurs Forward." Small Business Administration. May 2012. Retrieved from

http://www.sba.gov/sites/default/files/files/small_business_report_final.pdf.

3. "Bankruptcy Statistics." United States Courts. (2012). Retrieved from http://www.uscourts.gov/Statistics/BankruptcyStatistics.aspx. The rate of bankruptcies in the U.S. peaked in 2010, but has remained 20-40 percent higher than pre-2008 figures.

4. *Ibid.*

5. Shakespeare, William. *Henry IV, Part 2.* Ed. Maynard Mack. Penguin: New York, 1986.

6. Shane, Scott. "Hallmark of the Great Recession: Job Loss from Small Business Closure." *Forbes*. April 29, 2012.

7. *Ibid.*

8. *Ibid.*

9. Shane, Scott. "Jobs Lost From Company Failure a Small Business Problem." *Forbes*. May 26, 2012.

10. "Small Business Economy 2011." Small Business Administration, Office of Advocacy. Retrieved from http://www.sba.gov/sites/default/files/SBE_2011_2.pdf.

11. *Ibid.* Figure reflects small business loans of $1 million or less.
12. Jinzu Chen, Prakash Kannan, Prakash Loungani, and Bharat Trehan. "New Evidence on Cyclical and Structural Sources of Unemployment." *International Monetary Fund* (May 2011; wp/11/106)http//www.frbsf.org/publications/econ omics/papers/21011/wp11-17bk.pdf
13. Zimmerman, Eilene. "How Six Companies Failed to Survive 2010. *New York Times*. January 5, 2011.
14. World Development Indicators. "The Little Data Book on The Private Sector." The World Bank (published June 21, 2013).
15. Clifford, Stephanie, Motoko Rich, and William Neuman. "Companies Warn That Higher Prices Are Looming." *New York Times*. February 14, 2011. Retrieved from http://www.nytimes.com/2011/02/15/business/15prices.html?pagewanted=all.
16. Friedman and Mandelbaum, *That Used to Be Us.*
17. Farrell, Christopher. "Bankruptcy Reform Bites Back." *Bloomberg Businessweek*. October 28, 2007.

18. Bailey, Martin Neal, and Douglas J. Elliott. "The U.S. Financial and Economic Crisis: Where Does It Stand and Where Do We Go From Here?" The Brookings Institute. June 2009. Retrieved from http://www.brookings.edu/~/media/research/files/papers/2009/6/15%20economic%20crisis%20baily%20elliott/0615_economic_crisis_baily_elliott.

Chapter 4

1. Bernd Schmitt, *The Big Think Strategy: Leverage Bold Ideas and Leave Small Thinking Behind* (Harvard Business Review Press, 2007), 4.
2. London School of Economics, "Clear View of the Cloud: The Business impact of Cloud Computing," by Leslie Willcocks, Will Venters and Edgar A. Whitley. (August 2011).
3. Brian Tjemkes and Pepign Vos, *Strategic Alliance Management* (Routledge, 2012), 4.
4. For an online version of the DoD Guidebook, see their Office of Small Business Programs website: http://www.acq.osd.mil/osbp/docs/dod_OSBP_Guidebook_for_Facilitating_Small_Business_Team_Arrangements.pdf.

Notes

5. Carol Tice, "Six Business Trends to Watch This Year." *Entrepreneur Magazine* (January 4, 2013).

Chapter 5

1. Citation for: Senator John McCain, the Republican presidential nominee in 2008, remarked concerning the flow of money into lobbying and election campaigns as "nothing less than an elaborate influence-peddling scheme in which both parties conspire to stay in office by selling the country to the highest bidder." The New York Times title "The Long Run..McCain Self confidence on Ethics" by Jim Rutenberg, Marilyn W. Thompson, David D. Kirkpatrick and Stephen Labaton. February 21, 2008.

2. Saez, Emmanuel. "Striking it Richer: The Evolution of Top Incomes in the United States." (March 2, 2012). Retrieved from http://elsa.berkeley.edu/~saez/saez-UStopincomes-2010.pdf.

3. "Trends in the Distribution of Household Income Between 1979 and 2007." Congressional Budget Office. (October 2011) Retrieved from

4. Smith, Hedrick. *Who Stole the American Dream?* Random House: New York, (2012).
5. Chen, Jinzu, Prakash Kannan, Prakash Loungani, and Bharat Trehan. "New Evidence on Cyclical and Structural Sources of Unemployment." (March 2012).
6. Henrick Smith, *Who Stole The American Dream* (New York: Random House, 2012).
7. The Democratic Party's 2012 Platform." *Detroit Free Press*. (September 5, 2012). Retrieved from http://www.freep.com/article/20120905/NEWS15/309050067/The-Democratic-Party-s-2012-platform.
8. *Citizen United v. Federal Election Commission* was a landmark 2010 case in the United States Supreme Court that held that corporations and unions cannot be restricted by government with regard to their political contributions and expenditures due to the First Amendment rights.
9. Kadlec, Charles. "The Dangerous Myth about the Bill Clinton Tax Increase." *Forbes*. July 16, 2012. Retrieved from

http://www.cbo.gov/sites/default/files/cbofiles/attachments/10-25-HouseholdIncome.pdf.

Notes

http://www.forbes.com/sites/charleskadlec/2012/07/16/the-dangerous-myth-about-the-bill-clinton-tax-increase/.

10. Everett, Jim, and John Watson. "Small Business Failure and External Risk Factors." *Small Business Economics*, Vol. 11, No. 4. (December 1998).

11. Clifford, Catherine. "States with Worst Business Failure Rates." CNN Money. May 20, 2011. Retrieved from http://money.cnn.com/2011/05/19/smallbusiness/small_business_state_failure_rates/index.htm.

Chapter 6

1. *Harvard Business Review*, "The New Science of Viral Ads," 2012, Thales Teixeira.

2. *Wall Street Journal,* May 1, 2013. Amir Efrati, "You Tube Touts Viewer Growth to Advertisers."

3. EIU/Lyris, "Mind the Marketing Gap," http://www.lyris.com/us-en/eiu.

4. Jeff Roberts, "Pretty Enough for TV." *Wall Street Journal* (May 2, 2013).

5. *Wall Street Journal,* May 2, 2013, by Jeff Roberts, "Pretty enough for TV."

6. John Hazard, "Journalist Take Refuge in the land of Branded Content." http://www.theobserver.com (February 6, 2013).

Chapter 7

1. Aparna Mathur, "Forgive Us Our Debts," The American (http://www.american.com/archive/2007/january-february-magazine-contents/forgive-us-our-debts.)
2. Joseph Schumpeter, Austrian American Economist, noted for his studies of The Evolutionary Economics, Business Cycles and Democracy; reference "History of Economic Analysis."
3. "Did Bankruptcy Reform Increase Financial Distress?" NBER Digest, November 2007. Summary of "Bankruptcy Reform and Credit Cards".
4. *Journal of Legal Studies*, vol. 39:1 (January 2010), 33-61.
5. "Bankruptcy Reform and Credit Cards," NBER working paper 13265, August 2007. J. of Economic Perspectives, Fall 2007, pp. 175-199.

6. Bankruptcy Reform Gave Creditors Too Much," Opinion piece in Washington Post, online edition, August 21, 2006.

7. "Consumer Bankruptcy in the USA and in France," Economies publique/Public Economics, no. 18-19, pp. 3-27, 2006.

8. "A Confederacy of Lunches" by Christopher Buckley about Marke Leibovich's *This Town* in Sunday New York Times Book Review, Sunday July 28, 2013. And the book 'This Town: Two Parties and a Funeral-Plus Plenty of Valet Parking! In America's Gilded Capital" by Mark Lebovich, Published by Penguin Books copyright Mark Lebovich 2013.

9. *Journal of Legal Studies*, vol. 39: 1 (January 2010), 33-61.

10. "Did Bankruptcy Reform Increase Financial Distress?" NBER Digest, November 2007. Summary of "Bankruptcy Reform and Credit Cards".

11. Amy Bingham, "Donald Trump's Companies Filed for Bankruptcy 4 Times", ABC News, www. abcnew.go.com.

12. Thomas Freidman, "I Want to Be Mayor" (New York Times July 28, 2013).
13. Hillel L. Pressor, Esq., *Financial Self Defense* (Garrett Press, 2009).
14. Joseph A. Schumpeter, *Capitalism, Socialism, and Democracy* (London: George Allen and Unwin Publishers 1976).
15. *Ibid.*

Chapter 8

1. Eckhart Tolle, *The Power of Now* (Namaste Publishing and New World Library, 1999).

www.ingramcontent.com/pod-product-compliance
Lightning Source LLC
Chambersburg PA
CBHW051639170526
45167CB00001B/248